THE *Adoption*
SOURCEBOOK

THE

Adoption
SOURCEBOOK

A Complete Guide to the Complex Legal, Financial,
and Emotional Maze of Adoption

By
Cheryl Jones

Roxbury Park

LOWELL HOUSE JUVENILE

LOS ANGELES

NTC/Contemporary Publishing Group

Library of Congress Cataloging-in-Publication Data

Jones, Cheryl.
    The adoption sourcebook : a complete guide to the complex
legal, financial, and emotional maze of adoption / Cheryl Jones.
        p.   cm.
    "Roxbury Park book."
    Includes bibliographical references (p.   and index.
    ISBN 1-56565-906-6
    1. Adoption—United States—Handbooks, manuals, etc.   I.
Title.
HV875.55.J65 1998
362.73'4'0973—dc21   98-26801
                                                         CIP

Published by Lowell House
A division of NTC/Contemporary Publishing Group, Inc.
4255 West Touhy Avenue, Lincolnwood (Chicago), Illinois 60646-1975 U.S.A.

Requests for such permissions should be addressed to:
NTC/Contemporary Publishing Group, Inc.
4255 West Touhy Avenue, Lincolnwood (Chicago), Illinois 60646-1975 U.S.A.

Lowell House books can be purchased at special discounts when ordered in bulk for premi-
ums and special sales.
Contact Customer Service at the above address.

Managing Director and Publisher: Jack Artenstein
Editor in Chief, Roxbury Park Books: Michael Artenstein
Director of Publishing Services: Rena Copperman
Managing Editor: Lindsey Hay
Designer: S. Pomeroy

Roxbury Park is an imprint of Lowell House,
A division of NTC/Contemporary Publishing Group, Inc.

Printed and bound in the United States of America

10   9   8   7   6   5   4   3   2   1

*This book is dedicated to families and children
whose lives are touched by adoption and to those
who work to make loving homes a reality for everyone.*

Contents

Introduction

I have been involved in the adoption community for almost twenty years now. During that time, I have had the pleasure of seeing many children find loving homes. I have shared tears, joy, anger, disappointment, fear, anxiety, despair, and exhilaration with birth parents, adoptive parents, grandparents, foster parents, and children. I have experienced the highs and the lows and seen incredible strength of character displayed by everyone involved. People who are touched by adoption in any way are probably the nicest, kindest, most generous group one can find. I have been reminded over and over again that there is a force at work in our lives, guiding us, protecting us, and teaching us. Your own personal beliefs will dictate what you call this force. If you complete the adoption process, you will not, however, be able to deny its existence.

A children's book written by Ed Young (*Red Thread,* Philomel Books, 1993) relates a Chinese folktale that has special meaning for many adoptive parents. In the story, a young man who is looking for a wife visits with a matchmaker. The older man consults his book and tells the young man that his wife is only three years old and that he will not marry for fourteen more years. He goes on to explain that men and women are joined by an invisible red thread when they are born. Regardless of their social status or location, they will eventually marry if their feet are tied together with the red thread. The young man is fascinated and asks all about his bride-to-be. The matchmaker takes him to see her. When he sees that she is not very attractive and that

---

In April 1995, Ruthanne Timm and her husband, Don Siedhoff, took a leap of faith in accepting the referral of a seventeen-month-old Russian boy, based on one short paragraph of medical/social information and a photocopied enlargement of a tiny black and white photograph. They were told to expect to travel in two weeks to two months. However, a moratorium on Russian adoptions went into effect soon after they accepted the referral, and they began a long wait. In October, with no end in sight, as Ruthanne was lamenting the fact that their son was spending his second birthday in an orphanage, it suddenly hit her that he had been born on the exact same day two years ago that her mother had died. At that point, all the doubts and fears she had about the adoption dissolved completely. Today, when Andrew says "Oh, my goodness!" just like Ruthanne's mother did, she is certain that as one of the most important people in her life left this world, another was sent to take her place. When they first accepted Andrew's referral, Ruthanne and Don rushed to prepare one of their upstairs bedrooms for the nursery. There was a street light outside the bedroom window that was supposed to automatically turn itself off during the day. Instead, it burned continuously during the ten months they waited to travel to complete the adoption, shining into the room that was ready and waiting for their little boy. She feels it was a sign that her mother was watching over their adoption from Heaven and that everything would work out all right.
(Special thanks to Ruthanne Timm)

---

she is being carried through the marketplace by a half-blind woman, he becomes very angry and declares that he will never marry her. He then pays his servant to kill the girl. The servant goes to the marketplace, stabs the girl, and runs away. Fourteen years pass and the man, who is still single, becomes a successful judge. A governor who appreciates his talents arranges for him to marry his beautiful daughter. The man is ecstatic and looks forward to having a family of his own. After the marriage, he learns that his wife is actually not the daughter of the governor but the child he saw in the marketplace. Everything the matchmaker told him had come true. When he told the story to his wife, he said, "It is a wonder, isn't it, that our lives and our fortune are known so well in heaven."

Many adoptive families believe that the invisible red thread connects them with the child that was meant to be theirs. Their faith helps them to endure the pain, uncertainty, and frustrations of the adoption process. For many, the home study is a time to reflect upon one's life and the events that have led to the adoption. You may be surprised to find that situations that seemed to have little meaning at the time have played a major role in preparing you for the child you will eventually adopt. Of course, you may not be able to see the red thread at work until after you have your child, but don't ever doubt that it is there.

Mike and Jill Crowley were in the process of adopting a baby from the People's Republic of China. She had already found her red thread: "Mike and I had been thinking for some time about planting a specimen shade tree in our front yard. Several weeks ago, on a warm early October afternoon, we visited the Morton Arboretum and fell in love with ginkgo trees! The ginkgo tree is native to eastern China, and is readily available, easy to grow in our climate (outside Chicago), and very beautiful. We decided that come spring, we would plant a ginkgo tree in the front yard in honor of our daughter-to-be.

"Fast forward . . . Mike took the day off work and we took the train into the city to complete our dossier. First stop, the INS to pick up our I-171-H. Then on to the Cook County Clerk's office to have Mike's employment letter county sealed. Well, it turns out the notary had bought a new stamp, but never renewed her registration, so we were told we had to have the letter re-notarized first. We left and back-tracked a couple of blocks to our bank, where a sweet woman at the information desk re-notarized the document. On our way back to the County Clerk's office, something caught Mike's eye in the middle of the crosswalk at the very busy city intersection of Clark and Washington: There on the pavement was a single, fresh ginkgo leaf! He picked it up and brought it to me. We looked around—not a ginkgo tree in sight for blocks and blocks—I don't know of any in the downtown area, and I've lived here all my life! I said, 'It's a sign that we'll have no more snags, and we're nearly done!' We carefully slipped the leaf into the portfolio containing our documents and proceeded to obtain the last county seal. Then on to the Secretary of State. They wanted us to leave the documents and come back for them the next day because we were over the same-day limit of fourteen documents! I started misting up and explained that Mike had taken the day off from work, and we *really* wanted to be able to deliver our documents to the Chinese Consulate this afternoon, and one of the ladies from the business documents division said she'd take care of it for me while we waited! I thanked her profusely and we were on our way to have lunch near the consulate when we spotted a copy shop and decided to make our photocopies of the State Seals. We came out of the copy shop and . . . there on the sidewalk was another single ginkgo leaf! Again, not a ginkgo tree in sight! It was as if God was telling us, 'You're nearly there, just one last step!' We had lunch, dropped off our documents at the Consulate with time to spare, did some shopping, and took the train home. When we arrived home, there was a message on our machine that Mike's Aunt Pat had passed away that morning. I started to cry and said, 'She left us the trail of ginkgo leaves!' I was raised to believe that when one soul passes on, another is born. Maybe our daughter was born today? At least we know that her Great-Aunt Pat is watching over her tonight and every night until we are to be united with her."

Chapter 1

Preparing for Adoption

There are many reasons why people seek to adopt children. Some are childless due to infertility or by choice, some have children of one sex and desire a child of the opposite sex, and others simply want to expand their family. The characteristics and personalities of the children needing adoptive families are as many and as varied as those of the families seeking to adopt. Becoming a parent is a personal decision that should be made carefully, regardless of how you plan to accomplish your goal. It is important to be in touch with your own feelings as well as your individual strengths and capabilities as much as possible. Patience, determination, a sense of humor, and good coping skills will be required every step of the way. You have already taken the first step by opening this book.

THE DESIRE FOR A CHILD

Whether you are childless or already have children by birth or adoption, you are considering adoption because *you* want a child. There should be some element of selfishness in your desire in order to get you through the challenges of adoption and later on, parenting. It is wonderful and noble to think about all the things that you can do for or offer to a child but it is also necessary to be aware of how you hope that parenthood will fulfill your own needs. If possible, make a list of the reasons why you want a child and discuss them with your spouse or a close friend. Verbalizing your thoughts will help you to examine them carefully and make sure your expectations are realistic.

Anyone who is considering becoming a parent needs to take a look at their present lifestyle, their emotional makeup, their health and their financial situation, and imagine the impact a child would have on all these factors. It is advisable to take advantage of every opportunity you can to interact with children, through volunteer work,

---

David made a lasting impression on me when I was preparing the home study for him and Debbie to adopt their first child. We were discussing his motivation for adoption and all the struggles they had been through with their infertility treatments. He looked at me with tears in his eyes and quietly said, "Do you know why I really want to adopt a child? I want to have the experience one day of a child looking up at me and saying, 'Daddy, let's go get an ice cream.'" That statement let me know how sincerely he desired the simple pleasures of being a parent. He has since adopted two boys, Brandon and Taylor, and I have had the honor of being involved in both placements. It is obvious that he treasures his children and he doesn't let a day go by without saying, "I love you."

---

babysitting, or just visiting with friends and relatives. Any experience you can get will help you to formulate ideas about the changes that will occur in your life after a child arrives and also help you to understand normal child behavior. You can count on less sleep, less time for yourself, less order and organization in your household, and less money after you have a child. You can also count on deeper feelings of love, frustration, and pride than you ever dreamed possible, a totally different set of priorities, and the joy of looking at life through the eyes of a child. If you feel that the advantages outweigh the disadvantages, you are ready to get started.

If you are married, it may be that you and your partner are at different stages of readiness for parenting in general or for adoption. This is very common and is not an immediate cause for concern. Consider how the two of you have approached other major deci-

---

Susan had been asking her husband, Jim, to consider adopting a child for many years. Each time she brought it up, he said that he needed to think about it some more. They had one biological son and had been unable to have more children. Susan really wanted their son to have a sibling. She kept casually mentioning the possibility of adoption but never got much of a response from Jim. One Sunday morning, Jim arrived late at church and had to sit in the front pew. That particular day, an adoptive mother was speaking to the congregation about the need for families for children from other countries. Jim left the church, went home to get Susan, and took her back to meet the speaker. From that point on, he was an eager participant in the adoption process. When he was describing that Sunday morning to me, he said, "I felt as if God was shining a light on me and saying, 'You will go to China to adopt a child.'" After they brought their beautiful daughter home, Jim confided that they had such a wonderful experience with their adoption, he wished they had done it a lot sooner.

---

sions during your marriage, such as the purchase of a new home or acceptance of a new job in a different city. If your spouse is the type of person who needs to research every detail, give him or her the time and space to do so. This doesn't mean that you can't help the process along by checking out books from the library or posting notes on the refrigerator about upcoming adoption seminars in your community, it just means that you should respect individual differences and time frames. People who function on a more emotional and impulsive level may be frustrated by those who take careful, deliberate actions. There is value in both approaches and spouses usually balance one another out. Becoming a parent is a tremendous commitment and neither partner should be pushing the other into something for which he or she is not ready.

Many couples choose not to seek infertility treatments due to religious or philosophical beliefs. Still others choose adoption as their preferred method of family-building without attempting a pregnancy. Whatever your reasons, you should be secure in your decision and confident in your own ability to determine what is best for your family.

If you are single, you will have additional concerns which need to be addressed. These might include:

- How do you feel about day care?
- What is your support network?
- Will your financial situation allow you to cover your or your child's unexpected needs?
- How will you provide role models of the opposite sex for your child?
- How will parenting affect your plans, if any, to marry in the future?

These are just a few of the considerations a single parent must face, and it is important to think them through.

LOSS ISSUES

If you are like most people, you have had a fantasy child in your heart for many years, maybe even since you were a child. Your fantasy child has all of your positive characteristics and none of your shortcomings. He (or she) is beautiful, intelligent, athletic, kind, loving, and generous. He goes to bed on time, respects his elders, eats his vegetables, and best of all, adores his parents. Everyone has to reconcile their expectations to the reality of the children with whom they are eventually blessed. If you already have children in your family, you know that it is possible to love them unconditionally no matter how different they are from your fantasy child. Adoptive parents who have experienced infertility will need to begin to reconcile the loss of the fantasy child prior to starting the process of adoption. Theirs is a special burden because they are often struggling with these issues before they actually have a child, and the feelings of grief will be even more intense. If you have experienced the loss of a child through failed attempts at in vitro, miscarriage, or death, you will have had a more tangible event over which to grieve and may find it easier to work through your feelings. If you have never been pregnant, it may be a little more difficult for you to identify the stages of your grief.

Elizabeth Kübler-Ross, a well known psychiatrist and expert on death and dying, identified the following process through which most people pass following any loss or disappointment:

- *Denial.* You experience shock and numbness and hope that you will soon wake up and find out that everything has been a bad dream.
- *Anger.* You feel rage toward other people and/or toward your higher power for the injustice of the situation.

- *Bargaining.* You begin to think of ways that you might be able to change things or could have done something differently.
- *Despair.* You go through a period of depression during which you believe that things will never get better.
- *Acceptance.* You come to terms with your loss in a way that allows you to achieve a sense of peace and hope for the future.

The grief process is not an event but a cycle that you may experience many times throughout your life. If you have ever lost a loved one, you know that with time, your sense of sadness is less acute—but you may continue to feel especially sad from time to time, perhaps each year on the anniversary of the person's birthday. You don't stop thinking about them or loving them, it just isn't as painful. Similarly, the loss of the child that you would have had should be acknowledged and hopefully resolved to some extent before you turn your attention to adoption.

Getting Started

The following are some steps you will want to take to help you begin the journey toward being united with your son or daughter. You may have already done some of these while you were considering adoption.

Contact other adoptive parents   You will find that other adoptive parents will be your greatest source of support, encouragement, and information throughout the adoption process and later as your child grows up. The friendships you will form may last a lifetime and will be very beneficial to your child. If you have associates or friends who have already adopted, ask them to share their experiences with you.

Most adoptive parents are thrilled to be able to help others who are genuinely interested in adoption. If you meet someone in a public place and decide to approach them because their child appears to be adopted, be sure to let them know right away that your motivation for asking questions is your own interest in adoption. I have had many people relate stories of following families with foreign-born children through the mall trying to get up the courage to start a conversation. Most people are not offended if you communicate your intentions up front and let them know that you are not simply trying to satisfy your idle curiosity.

You can consult your state adoption specialist, your library, or perhaps your newspaper for information about adoptive parent support groups in your area. (There are listings of adoption specialists and support groups in chapter 11.) Attend a meeting or a seminar and try to talk to as many people as you can. You will probably find others who have a situation similar to yours, and it will make you feel less isolated and more confident to begin the search for an adoption professional.

Read books, magazines and newspapers Chapter 11 contains information about organizations that publish articles, newsletters, or magazines about adoption as well as sources for popular books on the subject. Adoptive Families of America publishes a bimonthly magazine that is an excellent source of information. Be careful—you will find yourself sitting down to read it from cover to cover without a break as soon as it arrives in your mailbox! The National Adoption Information Clearinghouse (NAIC) provides lots of articles and lists loaded with good information at no cost. Get suggestions from other people or simply browse through different books at your library or bookstore to see which ones appeal to you. Many newspapers now have searchable archives available on the Internet where you can look up past articles about adoption.

Do some research on the Internet There is information about many adoption-related websites listed in chapter 11. If you don't have a computer at home, take the time to find out where you can gain access to one. You may be able to go to a cyber café, a friend's house, or your local library. There is such a wealth of information available that you may find it overwhelming at first. There are websites for families who have adopted, birth parents who have made adoption plans for their children, agencies, professional organizations, and information clearinghouses. Keep in mind that not everything you will see on the Internet is true, so take the time to actually confirm the information with a number of sources before taking action.

Contact agencies or adoption professionals There are a number of organizations (see chapter 11) that provide listings of agencies, consultants, or attorneys all over the country. You can obtain one of those lists or get a list off the Internet. You might then call or write to various agencies for information packets. If you prefer to have some assistance in sorting through the various options and deciding which ones might be viable for you, many adoption agencies offer free orientation meetings. If your local agency doesn't have any actual adoption programs but only offers home study and postplacement services, it is possible that they will have brochures and fact sheets from child-placing agencies. If so, they can give you some ideas about the different programs that are available. Your adoptive parent support group may also be a good source of advice on how to select a program or an agency.

Some adoptive families find that it is helpful to use the services of an adoption consultant who is not affiliated with an agency. For a fee, the consultant may search a database for you and advise you about programs for which you qualify. You will receive a list of agencies and you will then contact those agencies directly. An adoption consultant may also be able to offer assistance and direction if you are pursuing an independent adoption, depending upon the laws of your state.

Contact attorneys   If you are planning to adopt a child through an agency, you probably will not need to contact an attorney until after a child has been placed in your home. You might want to ask the agency whether they can recommend attorneys in your area. If you are planning to adopt independently, you will want to contact an attorney as early in the process as possible. You can obtain a list of experienced adoption attorneys from your state Bar Association or the American Academy of Adoption Attorneys.

Important Points to Ponder

Everyone is different   You should not feel compelled to pursue a certain type of adoption because it worked for your sister or your friend. If you are uncomfortable with contact with birth parents or travel to a foreign country, for example, try to educate yourself as much as possible about the pros and cons involved. Give yourself (or your spouse) permission to rule out any situations that just don't feel right.

Be true to yourself   Consider your own personality and needs in making your adoption plans. If you are the type that is content to trust others to do their jobs competently, you will probably be happy working with almost anyone in your adoption efforts. If you need to be more in control and constantly aware of what is happening with your case, you will need to choose an agency or adoption professional that is responsive to your need to have some control. If you are the assertive, independent, adventurous type, you may be happy with a parent-initiated adoption where you do most of the legwork yourself. There are many different ways to become a parent through adoption, and one of them is sure to fit your own personal style.

Give yourself permission to feel ambivalent   Adoptive parents often expect to remain happy and optimistic throughout the entire process. There is a commonly-held notion that you are going to great lengths to become a parent and therefore you should never doubt or be unhappy about your decision. Nothing is farther from the truth. There will be many times when things don't go the way you anticipated and you may feel discouraged or depressed. If you have experienced infertility or the death of a child, you may be very reluctant to allow yourself to believe that you will ever be a parent. As the wait drags on, you may find that you need to detach yourself from the process in order to maintain your own sense of serenity. When you do have a child offered to you for placement, you might be surprised that you don't feel love at first sight. All of these emotions are normal and healthy. You will find that other adoptive parents or adoption professionals can help you through the rough spots.

Take as much time as you need in choosing an adoption professional The success of any journey is directly related to the adequacy of the preparations. You should view the adoption process as the most important journey of your life. Choosing your partners in the process is a very important step. The agency worker, consultant, attorney, or facilitator should be someone you basically like and can trust. If you feel intimidated or put off in your initial contacts, chances are the situation will not improve. It is okay to give someone the benefit of the doubt and talk to them several times to see if perhaps they were just having a bad day, but if your internal alarm system keeps telling you to beware, take heed. There will be many ups and downs in the process no matter how smoothly things go, and you want to be able to count on your adoption professional for support and understanding. It is very likely that you will want or need to be in contact with your adoption professional in the months or even years after your adoption takes place. If you don't develop a good relationship with that person, you might regret it for a long time to come.

If you are considering working with an adoption agency, check with the licensing officials in the state where the agency is located. Some states license adoption facilitators as well as agencies. If you are considering working with an attorney, check with the local Bar Association. In all cases, you can contact the Attorney General's office and the Better Business Bureau. References from recent clients of the adoption professional are also a very important means of finding out about their policies and practices.

Focus your energies on one option at a time   Each option for adopting a child requires a great deal of commitment in terms of time, money, and emotions. Many families enter the process feeling that they want to be on as many lists as possible so that they can accept the first available child. This sounds like a good argument but in reality it may not work out so well. If you have to make a financial investment in order to get on the various lists, you may lose a lot of money. More importantly, however, your emotional investment in each option will be great and you may become stressed out trying to keep track of different requirements, waiting times, fees, and responsibilities. There will be a lot of people involved in any process you choose and you may find it difficult to remember what each one told you and what your agreements have been with regard to responsibilities. You may also find yourself faced with some very tough decisions. If you have met with a birth mother and committed yourself to adopting her child, you will feel torn if someone calls you about another child who is already born and who is available for adoption. You will have to consider whether you want to adopt two children at once, whether the first birth mother will consent to your adoption if you have another child, whether your agency or your state allows placement of two unrelated children at the same time, and so on. It is a good idea to give yourself a realistic time limit during which you will devote all your attention to your chosen option. After that time has passed, reevaluate your situation and consider changing your strategy. Don't spread yourself too thin.

There are a few exceptions to this rule, especially in domestic adoptions. If you are on the waiting list with an agency that tells you that most families wait five to ten years to adopt a child, it is certainly advisable to pursue other options while waiting for your name to move up the list. Families who choose to network in order to locate a child to adopt never know when someone will respond to them. I have known many families who waited for months or even years after sending out letters to everyone they could think of, and then turned their efforts to agency adoption, and were later contacted by a birth mother and completed an independent adoption also.

There are few guarantees It is tempting to believe promises that you will hear during your quest for an adoption professional. However, there are many things that cannot be guaranteed. For example, an agency or facilitator can promise you that they will do everything in their power to obtain all the available medical information but they cannot guarantee that your child will be healthy. Similarly, they can promise that they will keep you informed of any new developments which might affect you but they cannot guarantee that your adoption will occur in a given period of time.

The only fees which can be guaranteed are those charged by the agency or other adoption professional for their services. Fees to be paid to anyone else are subject to change without notice and should be considered estimates only. In many cases, some of the fees charged by the agency will not be guaranteed until a child is actually accepted for placement. The home study fee, obviously, should not be increased during the home study process. It is, however, possible that the program fee will be increased prior to your actually signing the program agreement, usually after your home study is completed. Also, the fee for services related to the placement of a child may be subject to increase between the time of application and the time of child acceptance. Some people are dismayed by the fact that the total cost of the adoption seems to be a moving target and they can never really be sure that they have all the funds available.

Be very cautious about working with anyone who seems to make too many promises. It is always a good idea to talk to references, licensing officials, the bar association, or the Attorney General, as applicable, to find out if the individual or agency is reputable. There will always be a few unscrupulous individuals who will attempt to take advantage of hopeful adoptive parents. Be wary of agencies or adoption professionals who request most of the fee at the beginning of the process.

All adoptions are not the same Each adoption situation will be unique. You owe it to yourself and the child you will eventually adopt to work with professionals who have expertise in the area most beneficial to you. Not all attorneys are knowledgeable about adoption law and some may not be able to provide all the advice you need. Social workers who have had experience only in the area of domestic adoptions may not be able to offer the guidance you need in completing an international adoption. Whenever possible, surround yourself with people who have already been through the type of adoption you are hoping to complete.

You will need the assistance of many people in your adoption efforts
In every adoption, you will need the services of an agency (public or private) or social worker, and probably an attorney at some point. Even if you arrange an adoption on your own or through a facilitator, you will still need an agency to do the home study or the court report and, most likely, an attorney to represent you in court. You will need to find out about the costs involved in obtaining all the services you need before you commit to any particular program.

There will be a seemingly infinite number of people whose assistance you will need in one form or another, in addition to your adoption professional. Each piece of paper that is required will have to be signed, copied, and mailed. You will need the assistance of your local police department in obtaining the necessary fingerprints or criminal records check, and your doctor will need to prepare a report or letter for you (the nurse or office manager or all three may need to be involved, also), etc. There will be many events which have to happen over which you will have little control. It is helpful to try to remain optimistic and pleasant in your interactions with all the people you encounter. Set realistic goals and work diligently toward them. Allowing yourself to worry excessively about the little things will create a lot more stress in a process that is already very emotional and unpredictable. Many people find it essential to prepare a list of the things they need to do and prioritize them. Your adoption professional should be able to help you do that. Making a list that can be systematically followed helps promote a feeling of control.

CHOOSING A PATH

After you have done all the research you can and talked to as many people as possible, you will want to start narrowing down your choices. The first decision you will need to make will be whether you want to adopt a child domestically or internationally. Next, you will want to decide whether to adopt through an agency or to arrange an independent adoption with the assistance of a facilitator and/or an attorney. Finally, you will want to decide whether you prefer to adopt an infant or an older child. Many of these decisions will have been made during the course of your information gathering. The decision about the age of the child you hope to adopt may be delayed until you are actually in the home study process in some cases. The purpose of this book is to help you make informed decisions. Keep in mind that there are no "right" answers except what you feel to be the best alternative for you and your family. The following are some characteristics of various types of adoption to help you begin considering your options:

Domestic Adoption of Newborn Infants

- Adoption plans are usually voluntary.
- Birth parents may have a role in selecting adoptive parents.
- Birth parents may desire ongoing contact through letters, pictures, and personal visits.
- Children are usually placed in the adoptive home at a very young age, often within a few days of birth.
- Children may be placed in adoptive homes before the rights of the birth parents have been fully terminated, thus creating a legal risk situation.
- Family medical history is usually available.

- Children may not be of the same racial or ethnic background as the adoptive parents.

Domestic Adoption of Older Infants or Children

- Adoption plans may be voluntary or involuntary.
- Birth parents may desire ongoing contact.
- Foster parents or siblings may desire ongoing contact.
- Children may have experienced numerous moves and changes in caretakers.
- Family medical history may or may not be available.
- Children may be placed in adoptive homes before the rights of the birth parents have been fully terminated, thus creating a legal risk situation.
- Children may not be of the same racial or ethnic background as the adoptive parents.

International Adoption

- Adoption plans may be voluntary or involuntary.
- Contact with birth parents, foster parents, or others may be limited or impossible.
- Travel to a foreign country may be required.
- Children are usually at least several months old at the time of placement with the adoptive family due to the time needed to complete the necessary bureaucratic process.
- Children may have lived in an institution or experienced numerous moves and changes in caretakers.
- Family medical history may or may not be available.

- The rights of the birth parents will have been fully terminated prior to placement of the child in the adoptive home, although the placing agency may retain legal guardianship.
- Children may not be of the same racial or ethnic background as the adoptive parents.

ELIMINATING THE OPTIONS

There is no foolproof method for making decisions about adoption. You will need to gather all the available facts and evaluate the options carefully. In the end, however, your instincts will be your best guide to the route that will work for you.

It is natural to think that, by choosing one type of adoption over another, you are minimizing the risks involved or avoiding dealing with certain adoption-related issues later on. The reality is that all families formed through adoption will share some common experiences and emotions. All adoptive parents feel very vulnerable. One of the most intimate and important endeavors you will ever undertake, that of becoming parents, must be shared with people you have never met before. You may experience fear, anxiety, joy, excitement, anticipation, and disappointment all at the same time. You will be asked to make a commitment to love a child for the rest of your life regardless of what the future may hold for you or him. Families who are adopting children domestically cannot ignore adoption issues even though they are not faced with them on a daily basis like those who adopt internationally. Likewise, families who adopt internationally cannot ignore the existence of birth parents even though they don't have regular contacts with these parents. You should have a basic understanding of the special issues relative to adoption no matter which route you choose. A good support network to help you along the way is invaluable.

On a practical level, some of the major factors which must be considered in choosing an adoption route are time frames, costs, qualifications (age, marriage, family composition, religion, etc.), the characteristics of the children needing families, and requirements for travel. With some of these factors, there may be flexibility within the same agency or between agencies and programs. When you are gathering information, be sure to ask whether the requirements listed are guidelines or are based upon laws or policies which cannot be changed.

The decision of whether to use a traditional adoption agency or arrange your own adoption may be out of your hands in some cases. If you hope to adopt a newborn in the United States and you are in your forties, you may find that agencies will not accept your application because their waiting lists are already long and by the time you would be considered for a child you would have passed the age limit. Your location may limit your access to agencies because some only serve a certain geographic area, especially for the placement of healthy newborns. Your religious preference may also exclude you from the services of some agencies. Of course, you may simply be the type of person who prefers to take charge of things and finds it more appealing to be more actively involved in finding a child. There are some agencies that promote parent-initiated adoptions and provide guidance and support to families who then locate their own children to adopt.

Chapter 2

The Adoptive Home Study Evaluation

eing the subject of a home study can be especially intimidating. Prospective adoptive parents usually feel as though they are being judged and feel compelled to give the "right" answers or make a "good" impression. Most are relieved to learn that social workers are just normal people who can understand and appreciate individual differences. In most cases, the home study worker is not the person who is making the final decision about whether to place a child with a given family. His or her job is to prepare an objective report that represents the kind of life that a child placed in that home might have. The home study process itself is a tool for the adoptive parents because it helps them analyze their own backgrounds and their philosophies on family and child-rearing and allows them to evaluate their own readiness for parenting. The home study is a tool for placement agencies, child welfare officials, or birth parents because it provides them with the information they need to decide whether the needs of a specific child can best be met by a certain family.

In addition to assessment, education should be a major part of the home study process. Many agencies therefore offer or require attendance at conferences, seminars, or panel discussions to provide applicants with the opportunity to begin learning about the issues unique to families formed through adoption. Many people who grudgingly drag themselves to an all-day Saturday seminar end up hanging on every word and staying late to ask questions. Panels of young adult adoptees are especially helpful in giving you ideas about the kinds of struggles your child may face later on. If you use an individual practitioner or an agency that doesn't offer an educational component, you can explore other resources through your local adoptive parent group or a national organization such as the North American Council on Adoptable Children (NACAC).

In most cases, the home study is done prior to consideration of the applicants as prospective parents. However, some states allow for birth parents to arrange the placement of their child independently through an attorney or other third party and the home study is done only after the adoption petition has been filed in court.

THE CRITERIA

What makes the perfect parent? On the surface, this seems an easy question to answer, but actually it is extremely difficult on a case by case basis. We can all look around us and see the strengths and weaknesses of others' parenting skills. It is easy to agree that all children deserve to be raised by parents who can love them and provide for their basic needs. However, the responsibility for deciding whether or not a given person or couple is suited to adopt a child is daunting. The decision may be in the hands of a young birth mother or a middle-aged bureaucrat who come from very different backgrounds and have very different perceptions of life. For prospective adoptive parents, the imposition of criteria in the selection process often feels unfair. After all, if someone cannot or does not want to raise their child, shouldn't someone who genuinely wants a child be allowed to raise him? Unfortunately it's not that simple; the people involved in making decisions about a child's future have to use some type of criteria in order to feel secure about their actions and optimistic about the child's chances for a happy and fulfilling life. Rarely, if ever, does anyone involved in an adoption take these responsibilities lightly or walk away from a child without looking back. Think for a moment about a child whom you know and love. If you were faced with placing him with an adoptive family, what criteria would you use?

The criteria for adoption are established by the various entities involved (i.e. agencies, birth parents, courts, and state or federal governments here or abroad), depending upon the type of adoption being proposed. Some criteria will be clearly stated in the laws of a given state and others will be left to the discretion of the agencies and courts. Criteria are influenced by a number of factors, with the best interests of the child being paramount. Definitions of "best interests" vary greatly and are very subjective. Hopefully, criteria established by agencies, courts, and governments will be based upon sound professional research and accepted social work practice, although they may be influenced by things such as funding sources and personal philosophies of agency directors and/or lawmakers. To understand the criteria and how they are developed, it is helpful to consider who has the ultimate responsibility for the child's welfare and the perspective from which they are approaching the issue. A child welfare official in a developing country who is making a decision about placing a child in the United States may have a limited understanding of our culture and the resources available to cope with chronic medical conditions, for example. Hence, they may be less likely than a child welfare official in the United States to consider an applicant with Diabetes Mellitus to be a suitable candidate for adoption.

Characteristics that are usually evaluated include:

- age of prospective adoptive parents
- marital status

- length of marriage
- family composition
- health (mental and physical)
- employment history and financial status
- criminal record
- residency
- citizenship
- physical standards of the home

The parameters of these criteria will vary depending upon the type of adoption being pursued. All adoptive families must meet the minimum criteria established by the state in which they live. In some states, prospective adoptive families are required to become licensed as foster families first. Once the applicable state and federal guidelines have been met, additional criteria will be imposed by the birth parents, the placing agency, or the foreign government.

Application of the Criteria—Domestic Adoptions

In domestic adoptions of infants, criteria such as age, marital status, health, and financial status are most often determined by the child's birth parents. These decisions are very subjective and will be influenced by life experiences and values. A birth mother who was feeling really depressed about making an adoption plan for her child once told me that she definitely did not want her child to be raised in a Catholic family. She stated that if the child was a girl, she would want her to have the option of terminating an unplanned pregnancy. Of course, not all Catholics are opposed to abortion, and being of a different faith does not necessarily mean that someone would support abortion. This young woman may have felt very differently weeks or months after the birth of her child, but the only thing that mattered was how she felt at the time the adoption plan was being made.

Birth parents who are in their late teens or early twenties may view adoptive parents who are in their mid-forties to be too "old" for parenting since their own parents may be in that age group as well. Other birth parents will prefer adoptive parents who are similar to their own parents. Some birth parents will reason that they are making an adoption plan for their child so that they will not have to raise him/her alone and therefore they will not consider a single parent. Other birth parents are open to considering the single person's financial status, lifestyle, health, and support system such as extended family members before rejecting them as a prospective parent. Some birth parents want their child to be the first or only child and others want to make sure that the child will have siblings. I have worked with birth mothers who requested adoptive families who liked dogs and cats, lived in the city, lived in the country, liked music, or enjoyed traveling. Sometimes these requests were motivated by a desire for the child to grow up in a home similar to what they had and other times by a desire for the child to have something that they felt they had missed.

In domestic adoptions arranged by public or private agencies for children whose birth parents are not involved in the process, these criteria are often set by the agency's board of directors or the public authority which governs the agency. For example, decisions about the age of parents may be based upon the theory that a person probably would not have a child born to them after age forty-five, so adoptive parents should not be more than forty-five years older than the child they adopt. Length of marriage is almost always clearly defined, with minimums varying from one to five years. Requirements concerning family composition will vary depending upon the age and sex of the child the family is seeking to adopt. There is often more flexibility when prospective parents are seeking to adopt a child who is older than a toddler, part of a large sibling group, of minority heritage, or who has physical or mental disabilities. Preference is usually given to the child's foster parents, if any.

Application of the Criteria—International Adoptions

In international adoptions, there are, in many countries, specific laws which govern the age of adopting parents, acceptance of singles as adoptive parents, and length of marriage. The minimum age of twenty-five years is set by the U.S. Department of Justice Immigration and Naturalization Service (INS). In the People's Republic of China, for example, preference is given to applicants who are thirty-five years old and childless for the placement of healthy infants. In Korea, adoptive parents must be between twenty-five and forty-five years old. The decision to accept singles may be made by the government or by the child caring institution responsible for the child. For many, there is a feeling that a child who may spend his or her life in an institution if not adopted should be allowed the opportunity to have at least one parent. Of course, placing a child with a married couple does not ensure that he/she will have two parents who will live to see him/her to adulthood. In our society, as in many others around the world, there are lots of children growing up happy and healthy in single parent households.

Criteria regarding the health of prospective parents are usually applied on a more individualized basis. While some agencies or governmental entities are unwilling to consider any person with a chronic health condition, some allow applicants to present extensive medical information with regard to lifestyle, life expectancy, and ability to care for a child. In almost all cases, prospective parents who suffer from communicable or life-threatening diseases (such as AIDS) will be disqualified from adopting a child.

The federal government has specific guidelines for the content of home studies to be used in international adoptions. These include:

- Statement about the qualifications of the person preparing the study and a citation of the state law that allows the party to conduct the home study.
- At least one personal interview with each adult member of the household and at least one visit to the home.
- A description of the number and types of contacts with the adoptive family.
- Criminal background check for each adult in the home.
- Statement that each adult was specifically asked if they have a history of substance abuse, child abuse, sexual abuse, criminal activity, or domestic violence even if it did not result in a conviction.
- If the applicants have previously been rejected as adoptive parents or the subject of an unfavorable adoptive home study, prior studies must be submitted with a full explanation of why the current study is favorable.
- Summary of preplacement counseling given and opportunities for postplacement counseling.
- Evaluation of financial capability.
- Assessment of the physical, mental, and emotional stability of all adults in the household and a statement about their suitability to care for a child.
- Detailed description of the home and a statement about whether the accommodations meet applicable state requirements, if any.
- Statement about the willingness of the prospective adoptive parents to provide for a handicapped or special needs child, if applicable.

- Specific approval of the adoptive parents which includes the reasons for the approval and the specific number, age, sex, and nationality of the child/children they are approved to adopt.

Documents Needed in the Home Study Process

During the home study process, prospective adoptive parents can expect to be required to provide the following documents:

- Birth certificates
- Marriage certificate
- Proof of termination of previous marriages
- Proof of adoption of other children already in the home
- Medical reports completed within the last year for all members of the household
- Proof of income (1040 or W-2 form)
- Fingerprint cards or police clearance certificate for all adult members of the household
- Autobiographical information
- Names and addresses of references who can write letters on their behalf
- Proof of health insurance to cover the child

THE INTERVIEWS

Some agencies or adoption practitioners will require that all documents be submitted prior to scheduling the interviews. This policy serves two purposes. First, if there are criminal records, medical problems, or other factors which might affect the acceptance of the adoptive applicants, they can be discussed and resolved. Second, if there are significant delays with gathering the documents, there is not a long lapse of time between conducting the interviews and completing the report. Sometimes workers do not write a study until they have all the necessary paperwork and it is difficult to write an accurate report if several months have passed. Other agencies will schedule the interviews right away and let the adoptive parents submit their documents over the course of the home study process.

Some agencies require attendance at preadoption classes prior to scheduling the home study interviews. In other cases, attendance at classes or seminars will be requested but can occur at any time during or after the home study process itself. The benefits of these classes can be tremendous. The group setting allows prospective adoptive parents the opportunity to form relationships with other couples or singles who are going through the process. Often, issues which one might not have considered will be raised by other group members and stimulate thought or discussion. Attending group meetings may help to reduce feelings of isolation, especially if you have experienced infertility and have felt overwhelmed that everyone around you seems to be able to get pregnant without any effort. Preadoption classes are often lead by people who have already successfully adopted and who can offer lots of insights into life as an adoptive family.

The interview process may take a few days or several weeks, due in part to the laws of the state where the adoptive parents live. In Georgia, for example, there must be at least three interviews with at least five days in between each interview. In most states, applicants must be interviewed individually as well as together. The location of the interviews will vary depending upon the practitioner or agency, but at least one will be in the applicants' home. All members of the household should be present at the time of the home visit.

What Are They Looking For?

Emotional stability   Be prepared to discuss your childhood, your adulthood, your education and employment history, and your adult relationships. Think about your life experiences and how they have influenced your present beliefs and values. You might want to share information about people who have been important in your development such as grandparents, teachers, or close friends.

If you are now or have been receiving counseling, you will be asked to explain the problem that made you seek counseling and how it has been or is being resolved. If you are currently under the care of a mental health professional, a letter from him/her will probably be required. Don't be afraid to disclose information about yourself to the social worker; nobody is perfect. The important point to consider is how you have dealt with any challenges you have faced in your life. The ability to identify problems and seek help for them will be considered a strength in a prospective parent because it indicates that you will be able to seek any assistance your child may need. There have been studies in the past which showed that adopted children were more likely to be in therapy than the general population. While this assertion was used by some to prove that adopted children have more problems, it has also been argued that adoptive families are more likely to recognize the benefit of and utilize professional services.

Your actions will be a strong indicator of your emotional state. It is very important that you resolve, if possible, any anger or guilt associated with your infertility or previous failed adoption attempts before beginning the home study process. Adoption professionals are usually in the role of helping children to find loving homes and helping parents realize their dreams of having a family. Thus, the home study process should be a partnership where both parties benefit. When an applicant is still struggling with anger, for example, they may take a defensive stance with the home study worker on every little detail such as submitting paperwork correctly or scheduling interviews. When applicants appear argumentative and unreasonable, it is impossible to give adequate attention to the issues which must be covered in the home study. Most agencies or practitioners will ask that the applicants seek counseling elsewhere to resolve their issues before completing the home study. Such a recommendation does not mean that you will never be approved as an adoptive parent, it may simply mean that you need a little more time to complete the grief cycle.

Letters of reference are important in portraying your individual character and personality. When choosing people to write the letters, think carefully about those who know you well. It is much better to use close friends who have spent a lot of time with you and/or your family. They can tell about specific occasions when they have observed you demonstrating qualities such as kindness, generosity, or concern for others. The agency or practitioner may provide the reference with an outline to follow, which could include some or all of the following areas:

- Relationship with you (how long they have known you, in what capacity, etc.)
- Observations about your family life, values, and morals
- Observations of your interactions with children
- Your strengths or weaknesses as prospective adoptive parents
- Acceptance of a foreign-born or special needs child into your family and community, if applicable
- History of or potential for substance abuse

References may also be interviewed in person or over the telephone, in some cases. In general, references should be people who are not related to you. You may be allowed to also provide references from your relatives but they will not count toward the minimum number of letters needed. Reference letters are usually held in confidence, thereby giving the writer the freedom to make any comments they choose.

Health   Medical information will be required for all members of the household. If you have any medical conditions for which you are receiving treatment, you may need to provide a separate letter from your doctor which addresses those conditions. Issues to be discussed include the diagnosis, treatment, side effects of treatment, limitations to activities of daily living or life expectancy, and an assessment of your ability to care for a young child. Major health problems will not necessarily rule you out as an adoptive parent, but may limit your choices as to the programs or countries in which you will be accepted. Obesity is seen as a health concern by some agencies or child welfare officials, for instance.

Marital relationship   Both spouses will be asked about the strengths or weaknesses of their relationship. Communication styles, roles, decision-making, values, and methods of coping with crises will be addressed. It is not essential that both spouses be exactly alike in their thinking and actions; it is more important that they recognize their differences and find ways to complement one another. It does help, of course, if both spouses have similar values and goals and work well together as a team.

Previous marriages   All prior marriages must be documented and discussed. You should take time to evaluate, if you haven't already done so, some of the reasons why you chose that spouse and why the relationship didn't work out. It is not necessary to assign all the blame to the other person. It is okay to be naive, immature, or simply misguided. Try to identify areas in which you learned or grew from the experience and how it has affected your choice of your current spouse and/or your relationship.

Education and employment   You will be asked to provide factual information such as names of schools or places of employment as well as a subjective account of your experiences. Academic performance, participation in extra curricular activities, and how you chose your career path may be discussed. If you have had a history of job changes, you will want to explain why you have moved from one company to another or from one field to another. Some industries are such that people move frequently in order to advance in the field. If that is the case, make sure that you communicate it to the person writing your home study. It is always helpful to offer information about your skills and abilities and how they are used on your job. Be specific about your responsibilities and your future career goals.

Family of origin   You will be asked to discuss your relationship with your parents, siblings, grandparents, and other relatives, both as a child and now. Family traditions, celebration of holidays, methods of discipline, and religious and ethical values will probably be discussed. If you have informed your extended family about your adoption plans, tell about their reactions and their plans for the new child.

Other family members   All members of your household will be included in the home study process. If you already have children, they may be asked about their feelings about the proposed adoption. Don't worry if your four-year-old tells the social worker that he doesn't want a baby because they're too much trouble. Children, just like adults, go through periods of ambivalence about impending changes in their lives. Think about how different your actual parenting experiences have been from your expectations beforehand. There is no real way to prepare yourself for how exhilarating or how scary it might be until you actually go through it. It's really impossible for your children, no matter how old, to be able to fully comprehend and anticipate how another child will affect their lives. It is important, however, that you have included your children in your discussions about the adoption and given them the opportunity to mull it over and ask questions.

For an adopted child, the home study process can be especially meaningful because it gives him an idea of what his parents went through before he was placed in their home. Hopefully, it will be an exciting time of anticipation that will make him feel good about himself. It is a great opportunity to tell his adoption story again and again.

You will be asked to describe your children's personalities and your family life. Be prepared to give specific information about how you plan to provide for another child. Think about the impact that another child will have on your children and how you will handle sibling rivalry.

Philosophies of parenting and child rearing Most people will parent their children in a similar manner to the way they were parented, unless they make a conscious effort to do things differently. Think about the things your parents did that you really appreciate and would like to do for your child as well as areas where you might improve. With changing values and expectations in society at large, the child-rearing philosophies your parents used may have been perfectly acceptable in the fifties and sixties but not in the nineties. Many people raised in homes where children were expected to be seen and not heard have established families where even the youngest members are involved in family debates, decision-making, and discussions.

It may help to make a list of things that you feel are important for a parent to teach or instill in a child and then make a list of the ways in which you would accomplish those goals. If you want to teach a child to make his own decisions, for example, you need to be ready to let him make bad choices and fail. Hopefully, children will be allowed to learn the basic lessons of life in the security of their family rather than out in the world. Beverly, an adoptive parent with whom I worked, told me that her parents were very concerned about making sure that their children experienced the luxury of being children. Thus, they did not give them many responsibilities or opportunities to make their own decisions. As a result, she felt that she made more mistakes as a young adult because she was inexperienced at thinking through choices and possible consequences.

Discipline practices have varied greatly from one generation to another. Parents in the fifties and sixties routinely used spankings and stern verbal reprimands that are considered detrimental by today's standards. It is helpful to observe other parents you know and how they handle their children's behavior. Reading books is another way to gather the information needed to formulate your own plans for discipline. Parenting classes are offered in many churches, schools, and hospitals but you may not feel comfortable attending them until you actually have a child. Some states or agencies even require that adoptive parents sign a contract stating that they will not use physical punishment.

Child care plans should be considered in advance. If you already have children, you may have experience with the different types of child care available in your community and what worked best for your other children. If you don't have children, you might want to talk to your friends, neighbors, or coworkers to get suggestions. Keep in mind that what is right for one child may not be for another and changes can always be made.

You will probably be asked to consider what your plans would be for guardianship of your child in the event of your death. If possible, talk it over with any prospective guardians and get their consent. If you are adopting a child of a different racial or ethnic background or a child with mental or physical disabilities, it will be especially important that the people you choose will be able to raise your child in an atmosphere of acceptance and security.

One wonderful aspect of parenting is that there are as many "right" ways to raise a well-adjusted child as there are people in the world. Regardless of your own beliefs and expectations, there will be an expert somewhere who agrees with you and has written a book on the subject. Be prepared to throw all your plans and ideas out the window, however, once your child arrives and you have to deal with the reality of parenting. Trust your instincts for responding to your child's individual needs to the best of your ability.

Religion   You may be asked to write a statement of faith or to discuss your beliefs. If you are actively involved in a faith community, you might use your religious leader as a reference. Agencies that are sponsored by a religious organization may have requirements about participation in a particular faith. Be specific about your plans for sharing your faith with your child and your plans, if any, to expose him to other faiths.

Finances   You may provide a letter from your employer, a copy of your 1040 tax form, or paycheck stub as proof of income, depending upon the requirements of your agency or adoption practitioner. You will also be asked to prepare a net worth statement that includes your assets as well as your liabilities. Your monthly budget should be clearly described and should reflect that you have adequate finances to provide for another family member. Be sure to include information about your life insurance coverage, also. If you have a will, make sure that it specifically addresses adopted children. If you don't have a will, you will want to consider writing one prior to the placement of a child.

Health insurance coverage   Under the Health Insurance Portability and Accountability Act of 1996, all employers who offer group health insurance plans which provide benefits for dependent children must cover adopted children from the date of placement, including preexisting conditions. The employee must notify the insurance company in writing to add the child to the policy within thirty days of the placement or the adoption. Adoptive parents may need to submit a placement agreement from the agency or the attorney or a copy of the adoption decree to prove that they are responsible for the child's care and that he has been placed in their home for the purpose of adoption. In addition, the law mandates that employers cannot apply preexisting condition exclusions when a person moves from one job to another. Check with your health insurance representative to find out about coverage for an adopted child. If you are told that your child will not have the same benefits given to other dependents, don't be discouraged. Adoptive Families of America (AFA) can provide information about the appropriate legislation that will help you in advocating for your child's rights to insurance benefits. Many agencies will ask you to provide a written statement from your insurance company regarding coverage for an adopted child.

Home and community   You will be asked to provide information about the resources available in your community such as hospitals, schools, libraries, and parks. If you are active in community organizations or clubs, include details about those. You will also be asked about the racial and ethnic makeup of the immediate area and how you feel an adopted child might be accepted.

The social worker will need to tour your home so he/she can write an accurate description and do a safety inspection. Some states have specific requirements about the physical standards of the home, for example, the placement of smoke alarms. You will want to have a plan for where your new child will sleep, even if you haven't converted that cluttered extra bedroom into a nursery. Some states have specific requirements about children sharing rooms, and in a few states each child must have his own room. In others, it may not be acceptable for children of different sexes to share a room after a certain age. If you have pets, you might be asked to provide evidence that they have been properly immunized.

Child request Depending upon the situation, adoptive parents may be able to request to adopt a child of a specific sex. Some agencies will require families who don't have any children or who have children of both sexes to be open to a child of either sex. For obvious reasons, parents who are seeking to adopt a child independently through a domestic adoption must be open to a child of either sex. There seems to be a tendency for adoptive parents to request a girl when allowed a gender preference. The basis for this trend is somewhat puzzling and there are several theories that have been used to explain it. One is that many people feel that girls are more compliant and therefore easier to raise than boys. Another is that men who are infertile are threatened by the idea that their son will be more "macho" because he may be able to father a child. Yet another is that the extended family would not want an adopted child, especially a foreign-born child, to carry on the family name. Regardless of the reasons, many agencies have been forced to place limitations on gender preference just to make sure that little boys do not wait longer than necessary for families.

The age of the child requested will be determined by applicable legal or agency guidelines. If there are restrictions with regard to the age difference between parent and child, for example, it might be necessary for parents over forty to be open to parenting a child who is older than two. The present family composition will also be taken into consideration. Some adoption professionals will recommend against adopting a child who is older than the oldest child already in the family or a child who is the same age and sex as another child. All families are different, however, and for some, the less than "optimal" age-spacing works out beautifully. Don't lose faith in your own instincts about what is right for your family.

Many agencies use medical condition checklists or questionnaires to help you determine your readiness to parent any child. These lists can be confusing and even frightening. It is very important to be truthful and to consider your answers carefully. If possible, go over the list with your doctor or another health care professional to make sure that you understand the conditions. Of course, no human being fits neatly into the categories listed, and for each condition, there will be varying degrees of severity. While it is tempting to answer "yes" or "maybe" when asked to consider most of the conditions, it is not in your best interests to do so unless you are emotionally prepared to seriously consider any child that might be offered to you for placement.

Many adoptive parents really struggle with their child request. I have heard people say they feel that they are playing God if they say "no" to an adoptive child because if they had a child by birth, they would love and care for the child regardless of their medical condition. It is a devastating experience for most prospective adoptive parents to have to turn down a child. It is also difficult for the birth parents and the adoption professionals involved. Educating yourself about various health concerns and the resources available in your area, carefully evaluating the personalities and needs of all family members, and being honest with your social worker can help to prevent you from being faced with a situation where you have to say "no."

Preparation for adoptive parenting The home study worker will need to make a recommendation about your suitability to parent the child that you are requesting. If you are planning to adopt an infant domestically, you might be asked to take infant CPR and infant care classes through your local hospital, for example. If you are planning to adopt an older child domestically, you might be asked to complete an extensive training course such as Model Approach to Partnerships in Parenting. If you are planning to adopt a child internationally, you might be asked to develop specific plans to help the child preserve his cultural heritage and expose him to role models from his country of origin. A thorough home study will include discussion of issues pertinent to your situation, such as dealing with birth parents, sharing the child's history, traveling to a foreign country, etc. It is not necessary that you have all the answers at this point, but a willingness to learn and a commitment to giving your child opportunities to explore issues related to adoption are vital.

Agency or Independent Practitioner?

Depending upon the state, home studies may be conducted by private individuals or persons affiliated with a licensed child-placing agency. Private individuals are usually licensed or otherwise certified by the state to prepare adoptive home studies. Check with your state licensing officials or your local court for a list of people or agencies qualified to conduct home studies. There are instances, however rare, where individuals prepare home studies for would-be adoptive parents even though the state they live in does not allow private home study preparation.

Some families feel that the following are advantages of using a private practitioner over an agency:

Flexibility The practitioner may be willing to schedule interviews in the evening or on the weekends rather than during normal business hours. If it is difficult for you to take time off from your job or if you travel a lot, such flexibility of scheduling may be essential.

Costs The fees may be lower since there are fewer administrative costs such as office rent, clerical staff, and the like.

Fewer requirements Attendance at classes or seminars may not be required when working with an individual.

Others feel that the following are the advantages to securing home study services from an agency rather than an individual:

Accountability Adoption agencies are required by state licensing officials to follow certain ethical standards of practice. It is usually required that all fees be disclosed in advance, for example. Agencies cannot then charge fees in addition to those agreed upon. A private practitioner may not be subject to the scrutiny of licensing officials and may be less accountable. If promises are not kept or deadlines not met, you may have less recourse with an individual.

Versatility When working with an adoption agency, there will often be many staff members that handle your case. If there is a conflict of personalities or philosophies, you can ask to be assigned to a different worker.

Resources With an agency, you can draw on the collective experience of *all* staff members. If your social worker has not encountered the specific situation in which you find yourself, there is a good chance that someone else in the organization has and can offer sound advice. Many agencies can offer classes or opportunities to be involved in adoptive parent support groups to help you prepare for adoptive parenthood.

Questions to Ask

Once you have a list of licensed agencies or individuals, contact them to ask the following questions:

What fees are involved and what do they cover?   Home study fees sometimes include postplacement visits and reports. When comparing one agency or practitioner to another, make sure that you know exactly what services will be provided. Another issue that frequently arises is the need for revision or update. If there is a major change in the composition of your household, a change of residence, or a change of employment, a home study update will, in most cases, be necessary. If a year passes and a child has not been placed in your home, an update may be necessary. In cases where adoptive parents have a home study prepared to adopt a child in one country and later choose to pursue another route, the home study will have to be revised. It is a good idea to find out ahead of time whether updates and/or revisions will result in additional expense.

How are fees paid?   Sometimes, the total fee can be paid in installments over the course of the interviews rather than in one lump sum in advance. In most cases, fees paid for home study services are not refundable. If something happens during the process such as loss of employment, job transfer, pregnancy, or illness that causes you to need to terminate the study, you will not lose as much money if you are paying the fee in installments.

How long will it take? Part of the answer to this question will depend upon you and your ability to collect and submit the necessary documents in a timely manner. It will also depend on your availability for interviews (people whose jobs require a lot of travel may need social workers who can meet them on the weekends). The other part of the equation is the current workload of the agency or individual. If there are staff shortages or if a holiday period is coming up, it may take longer to complete the study. It is also important to ask whether your study will be conducted by someone who works another full-time job and does home studies on the side or by someone for whom it is their major occupation.

What are the qualifications and experience of the person who will prepare the study? Since the home study process should be educational, adoptive parents will usually benefit more from having a worker who is experienced in the field of adoption.

Can I read the report before it is approved? The home study is probably the most critical element of your adoption paperwork and you will be anxious to make sure that it gives a good impression. Fortunately, it is common practice that adoptive families are given the opportunity to read the study before it is sent to the various parties involved in the adoption. There may be typographical errors that are not easily noticed except by the subject of the study. If your birth date is off by ten years, for example, you would see it right away. It is practically impossible for the person writing the study to cover everything in detail during the interviews and take adequate notes. Therefore, there may be areas where something is not explained accurately or information is misinterpreted. If you feel that something is not clear or creates a negative impression, discuss it with your social worker and suggest possible solutions.

Important Considerations Before Starting a Home Study

Where do you hope to adopt? Before you actually start the home study, you should have narrowed down your adoption plans as much as possible. The issues that will be important in a domestic home study will not necessarily be covered in an international home study and vice versa. If you are adopting a child internationally, some countries have their own preferences for the format of the home study and the issues that need to be addressed. The child welfare officials in the other country will want to see a discussion of why you want a child from their country and how you plan to instill pride in the child' s heritage. This does not mean that your home study cannot be amended or revised if you change from one program to another, it is just easier for everyone involved if you have a clear idea of how the study will be used before it is written.

Another factor to consider is the acceptance of home studies by different agencies. In some cases, placement agencies work with a network of partner agencies in states other than those where they are licensed. If you decide to adopt a child through a given agency and they have a partner or cooperating agency in your state, the placement agency may not accept a home study done by any other agency. If you are adopting through an agency that is licensed in your state, they will almost certainly require that your home study be prepared by their staff. It might seem that the agency only wants to make you spend more money for their services, but the real reason should be making sure that you receive adequate preparation for adoptive parenthood. Placement agencies need to feel confident about the quality of the services that you received as part of the home study. Agencies that work in cooperation with one another usually have similar standards of practice and staff qualifications. The placement agency may provide in-service training for the staff of the home study agencies. Good preparation is a key element in preventing adoption disruptions.

Do you have factors that might be problematic? If you are concerned about anything in your life, past or present, which may be considered a problem, it is best to discuss it with the parties involved at the beginning. Areas of concern might include previous marriages, health problems, unstable job history, arrest record, mental illness, or a lifestyle that is outside the norm. Agencies are often required by state law to provide families with the opportunity for orientation to the adoption process prior to filing an application. You should be able to talk to someone on the telephone or meet in person, if you prefer, to discuss your situation. If you are using two agencies, you need to clear it with the placement agency first and then the home study agency. If the placement agency does not feel that it is a problem, you can then approach the home study agency to find out how they will handle the report. If you do not get the response you want, you may be able to use another home study agency.

Of course, in many cases, the final decision is not up to the agency but rather to the birth parents or a foreign child welfare official. You can and should ask if the agency has ever worked with an adoptive family with similar circumstances and what the outcome was. They may be able to consult with their staff overseas, if applicable, to attempt to determine how the situation might be viewed given local customs and values. There is no way, of course, to predict how birth mothers who might be considering your family will feel about it. If your agency has not had any experience with a similar situation or if it is a new program, you may not have any good indicators on which to base your decision. There are risks inherent in any adoption and you may just need to rely on faith to proceed.

Chapter 3

Finances

*C*ost is probably the single most misunderstood concept in connection with an adoption. Adoptive parents often find strangers innocently asking them, "Well, how much did he cost?" During my years as an adoption worker, I have had some people comment to me that charging fees for adoption services is "baby-selling." Everyone, most adoption professionals included, would like adoptions to be free; after all, people who want children are providing homes for children who would not otherwise have them. If only it were that simple. Every society has laws in place which are supposed to protect the rights of its most vulnerable citizens, the children. The act of legally moving a child from one home into another necessitates that every possible measure be taken to ensure that he or she is not abused or jeopardized in any way. The costs associated with the adoption process cover the services provided by a variety of individuals or organizations to make sure that all the appropriate safeguards are in place. It is very important to keep in mind that you are paying for services, not for a child. It is also important to realize that, regardless of the route you choose, you may need the services of more than one adoption professional. If you adopt a child through an agency, you may still need an attorney to assist you with finalization. If you adopt a child through a facilitator, you may still need an agency (for the home study) and an attorney (for finalization of the adoption).

Examples of services that may be provided include:

- Professional services of an agency, attorney, or facilitator
- Medical care for the mother or the child
- Housing for the mother and/or the child
- Foster care for the mother and/or the child
- Court fees
- Travel expenses for the adoptive parents or an escort and the child
- Fees for issuance of a birth certificate, passport and/or U.S. Immigrant visa

Depending on your circumstances, you may need to pay only a few of these fees. Remember, however, that less is not always better. Adoption is a very complicated process from every side of the triangle and the support of experienced professionals often benefits everyone involved.

When investigating sources for assistance with your adoption plans, ask for a detailed list of all fees and when they are due. Make every attempt to understand exactly what the fees cover and who will handle various aspects of the process. It is very difficult to anticipate in advance what problems or challenges may arise and whose responsibility it will be to resolve them. For example, if you engage the services of an adoption agency only to prepare a home study, the agency staff may not be available to assist you when you have questions about U.S. Immigration requirements or when a birth mother calls you with a set of circumstances which you feel ill-equipped to handle. Ask the agency or facilitator to give you a detailed list of costs that you might expect to incur that aren't included in their fees. It is very helpful to talk with other adoptive parents to get an idea of important issues to take into consideration when evaluating fees. Although every adoption will be unique, others who have gone before you can give you invaluable insight which can help you make an informed decision. Even if you don't feel that you will ever have the need for certain services, make sure that you find out what services are offered, just in case.

Each step of the adoption process is a commitment of time, money, and emotions. There are no guarantees for a successful outcome regardless of the route you choose. It does help, however, to be an informed consumer and to understand the responsibilities of all parties involved. By talking to others (adoptive parents or adoption professionals), you can get an idea of what the normal costs are for the type of adoption you are considering and how the fees are usually paid. If information you receive from a facilitator or agency seems out of line, try to find out the reasons for the discrepancy. It is a good idea to be wary of any agency or professional that requires a large sum of money in advance. Adoption professionals should be willing and able to answer questions about fees and services. If you get answers that are vague or contradictory, ask for clarification or consider working with someone else.

Each state has its own laws governing the fees that can be paid in connection with an adoption. Such legislation is generally aimed at preventing the buying and selling of children. However, it also protects adoptive parents from future allegations by the birth parents that they were influenced to make an adoption plan by financial incentives. In some states, only licensed child-placing agencies are allowed to pay housing and miscellaneous expenses incurred by the birth mother during her pregnancy. If you are considering a private or independent adoption, it is a good idea to find out ahead of time what your state laws are with regard to payment of living expenses. If you eventually meet a birth mother who needs some assistance with housing or medical expenses and you cannot provide the funds directly or through your attorney, you will incur the additional expense of an agency for administration of the funds. It is customary that both the birth mother and the adoptive parents sign affidavits regarding any monetary exchanges to be filed in support of the petition for adoption.

VARIATIONS IN COSTS BY TYPE OF ADOPTION
All Adoptions

You need to include in your adoption budget the costs for obtaining all the documents needed for your home study. All adoptive parents will be asked to submit medical reports or letters from their doctor. There will, of course, be costs associated with medical exams, lab work, and other tests. There will, in most cases, be a fee to have fingerprint cards prepared and/or to have a criminal records or child abuse check done by the local authorities. You may have to order certified copies of birth, marriage, and divorce records and there will be costs associated with that.

You will also need to consider the costs involved in preparing to care for a child. You will need to have the basics such as furniture, clothes, and toys prior to or soon after your child's arrival. If your child has special needs, you may need to plan for home renovation or the purchase of special equipment. Of course, you will probably have plenty of friends and relatives who are willing and eager to help.

Private Agency Adoption

Adoption agencies typically charge a set fee for their services in connection with an adoption. The total fee may be made up of several smaller fees that are paid over the course of several months or years, depending upon how long the adoption takes. Fees are, in many cases, not refundable. Some states require that all fees and refund policies be outlined in writing and agreed to by the adoptive parents prior to engaging the services of the agency. Examples of fees include:

Registration fee   Usually a nominal fee of $25 to $100 to cover the costs of sending out initial information packets and handling inquiries from people seeking to adopt.

Application fee   Usually ranges from $100 to $2,500 and is used to cover the costs of providing the adoptive family with specific information regarding a particular adoption program, staff time, and general office expenses for file maintenance.

Home study fee   Usually ranges from $500 to $3,000 and is used to cover the costs of interviewing the prospective parents, traveling to their home, contacting references, conducting criminal records checks, writing the report, and forwarding it to the appropriate authorities. Agencies that are working with adoptive parents living in a state other than one in which they are licensed may charge a home study review fee for evaluating a home study prepared by another agency or social worker and making sure that it meets all applicable requirements.

Program fee   This fee may be broken down into several parts, depending upon the type of adoption being sought. Program fees may range from $2,000 to $25,000. In international adoptions, there may be one fee to cover the services of the domestic agency's staff and a separate fee to cover the services of the foreign staff or facilitator. The former is generally paid when the home study is approved and the agency begins working toward selecting a child who can be placed with the family. The latter is typically paid when a child is accepted for placement. You will also incur fees for certification and authentication of documents, filing INS forms, travel costs, foster care and/or medical care for the child, orphanage donations, etc. In domestic adoptions, an initial payment may be made prior to the agency sharing the family's profile with prospective birth mothers and the balance paid at the time a child is placed. Types of services included in this fee may be counseling for the birth mother and father and members of their immediate families, contacts with physicians or other health-care professionals, foster care for the mother and/or child, and facilitation of pre- or postplacement visits between the birth and adoptive parents.

Agencies routinely provide services to many birth parents who do not make an adoption plan for their children. The costs of these services must be built-in to the agency's fees. Thus, adoptive parents are paying a fee that is the average of the cost of services provided to all birth parents served by the agency rather than the cost of services provided to their child's birth mother. It can seem quite unfair to the family who knows that their child's birth mother only contacted the agency days before the child's birth as opposed to months in advance. However, agency fees are designed to ensure that the agency will be able to continue to provide services to all members of the triad in the years to come. Especially with the trend toward openness in adoption, birth and adoptive families are relying more and more on agency staff to provide ongoing liaison services and counseling.

Postplacement services Usually range from $200 to $2,000, depending upon the number of visits required. State laws often specify the frequency of visits prior to filing of the adoption decree. In international adoptions, families need to satisfy the requirements of their state as well as the foreign government. In cases where the adoptive parents travel overseas to finalize the adoption, the requirement for postplacement services may not be legally enforceable, but it is crucial to future adoptions that foreign governments receive documentation of how the children fared in their new homes.

Private or Independent Adoption

Adoptive families engaging in private domestic adoptions through attorneys or facilitators should expect to pay for the services of the professionals involved as well as out-of-pocket expenses. Professional services may range from $1,000 to $25,000 or more. Some states limit the amount of money that an attorney or other facilitator can charge. In a domestic adoption, the attorney may charge a set fee for handling the case plus an hourly rate for telephone contacts with the adoptive parents, the birth parents, the physician or hospital, etc. If you are adopting a child in another state, you will need to pay for the filing of the appropriate paperwork and follow-up telephone contacts with the Interstate Compact Administrator in the other state as well as your own. If you seek to locate a child to adopt through advertising or networking, you will incur all expenses involved. Sometimes, families have a separate telephone line with an 800 number installed in their home to take calls from birth parents. In contrast to adoptions through agencies, adoptive families may incur many expenses in connection with the birth of a child that they are not ultimately able to adopt due to medical complications or a change of plans on the part of the birth parents. It is for this reason that it is very difficult to predict ahead of time what the costs will be, and private adoptions have the potential for being more costly than agency adoptions.

If you are adopting a child internationally, you will need to pay for communication with the contacts in the foreign country through mail, telephone, fax, or e-mail in addition to the costs of medical care and housing (foster care or institutional care) for the child, authentication of documents, translations, and travel. If you are required to travel to the child's country to complete the adoption, you can expect to pay for the services of an interpreter/guide as well.

Even if you are completing an independent adoption, you may still need the services of an adoption agency for specific parts of the process. Some states allow their public social services departments to provide home studies and court reports in connection with private adoptions and others do not. Check with your state adoption specialist to find out where you can secure the services you need. Even if you can use the services of a public agency, you may find that the waiting times are too lengthy. Due to the limited resources available to most public agencies, services to children who are presently in foster homes or other publicly-funded care will receive priority over services to children who are being adopted privately.

Public Agency Adoption

In many cases, especially those involving waiting children, public agencies do not charge any fees for adoption services. If there are fees involved, it is possible that you will be charged on a sliding fee scale based upon your household income.

International Adoption

If you adopt a child internationally, anticipate the following fees:

Immigration and Naturalization Service (INS) fee All persons seeking to adopt a child in another country and bring him to the

United States will incur the expense of obtaining an immigrant visa for the child. At the time of this writing the fee for filing an I-600A (Application for Advance Processing of an Orphan Petition) or an I-600 (Petition to Classify Orphan as an Immediate Relative) is $155 plus $25 per adult for fingerprints to be taken by an INS-approved office. The fee for filing the form OF 230 (visa application) is now $260 plus a $65 fee for issuance of the visa. The fee for filing an N-643 (Application for Certificate of Citizenship in Behalf of An Adopted Child) is now $80 but is expected to increase to $125. Please see chapter 4 for an explanation of these forms and supporting documentation.

Document authentication fees   Child welfare officials in the child's home country may require a dossier or set of documents which provides evidence that the applicants can provide a suitable home for a child. A detailed description of a dossier can be found in chapter 4. Documents being used in another country must be authenticated or otherwise legalized prior to presentation overseas. Depending upon the origin of the document and the country in which it is going to be used, the costs may range from a few dollars to $75 per document.

Document preparation services   If the agency or facilitator does not assist you with obtaining the necessary certification and authentication of your documents, you may choose to use the services of a dossier preparation service to actually obtain your vital records and have all of your documents certified and authenticated by the appropriate authorities. The costs of these services will vary depending upon the complexity of the dossier and the amount of time involved. A general estimate would be from $200 to $500.

Translations   All documents must be translated into the language of the country in which they are going to be used. The translation fee may be included in the fee charged by the agency or facilitator. In some countries, translations can only be provided by persons who have been recognized as competent translator in that country. Generally, translation fees range from $300 to $1,000.

Travel costs   If you are required to travel to the child's home country to finalize the adoption, you will incur airfare, lodging, transportation, and other incidental expenses such as airport departure taxes. The adoption procedures in some countries necessitate either an extended stay or two trips. If you are not required to travel to the child's home country, you will still incur the cost of providing for an escort to bring the child to the United States. Airfares for children vary depending upon the age of the child. For infants under two, the cost is usually about 10 percent of the normal adult fare. For children age two to twelve, the fare is usually about 50 percent of the adult fare. If you want to reserve a seat for a child under two, most airlines will require that you purchase a ticket at the fare charged for a child over two.

Foster care or institutional care   You may be asked to pay for foster care on a monthly basis or to make a lump sum payment to the orphanage or other institution that provided for your child's care.

Medical care for the child   The costs for medical care are often included in either the agency's program fee or the fee for foster or institutional care. Your family medical insurance will most likely not cover medical care your child receives prior to placement in your custody. Ask your agency or facilitator what arrangements are made for medical care and whether or not you will be expected to assume all costs. Most of the time, medical care is far less expensive in other countries than it is in the United States, and your adoption professional should be able to give you an estimate of what to expect for routine medical care.

EMPLOYER ADOPTION BENEFITS

More and more employers are providing adoption benefits which create a family-friendly environment and make family-building more equitable. These benefits might include: reimbursement of adoption expenses, leave of absence (paid or unpaid), and resource and referral services. Provision of such benefits is cost-effective for employers because there is a relatively low utilization rate (more employees give birth than adopt). It also helps to strengthen morale and employee loyalty. If your employer does not offer adoption benefits, you can contact the National Adoption Center at 1-800-TO-ADOPT for information on advocacy strategies.

ADOPTION TAX CREDIT

The Small Business Job Protection Act (P.L. 104-188) became effective on January 1, 1997. It is very important legislation for adoptive families since it provides for an income tax credit of up to $5,000 ($6,000 for the adoption of U.S. special needs children) for parents as well as a tax exemption for employer-reimbursed adoption expenses. The credit and the exemption expire on December 31, 2001. If you have specific questions about your eligibility, you can contact the Internal Revenue Service (IRS) at 1-800-829-1040. Forms can be obtained by calling 1-800-829-3676. Forms and publications can be found on the worldwide web at http://www.irs.ustreas.gov.

Definitions

- A tax credit is a dollar-for-dollar reduction in a family's income tax liability. It is not the same as a deduction, which only reduces taxable income.
- An exclusion refers to the ability to exempt the amount received from your employer toward adoption expenses from your adjusted gross income (AGI). You will, however, be required to pay Social Security, Medicare tax, and unemployment taxes on these employer payments.
- The adoption tax credit covers qualifying expenses in connection with an adoption or an anticipated adoption.
- Qualifying expenses include "reasonable and necessary adoption fees, court costs, attorney fees, traveling expenses (including amounts spent for meals and lodging) while away from home, and other expenses directly related to, and whose principal purpose is for, the legal adoption of an eligible child." (IRS publication No. 968)
- An eligible child must be "less than 18 years old, or physically, or mentally incapable of caring for himself or herself."
- A special needs child must be a citizen or resident of the United States or its possessions when the adoption is initiated. The state where the child lives must establish that he or she cannot or should not be returned to his or her family of origin and that he or she probably will not be adopted unless adoption assistance is provided.

Limits

- A foreign-born child cannot be considered a special needs child.

- Expenses incurred in connection with stepparent adoptions or surrogate parenting arrangements are not considered qualifying expenses.
- The adoption tax credit does not cover adoption expenses which were paid using funds from a local, state, or federal adoption program, allowed as a credit or a deduction under any other federal income tax rule, or paid or reimbursed by your employer.

Dollar and Income Limits

- The maximum allowable benefit of $5,000 ($6,000 for U.S. special needs children) per child for the tax credit or the exclusion can only be taken by families whose AGI is $75,000 or less.
- For families with an AGI between $75,000 and $115,000, the credit or exclusion is reduced based upon the amount of income.
- Families with an AGI of more than $115,000 are not eligible for the adoption tax credit or the exclusion.

OTHER IMPORTANT POINTS

- If you qualify for a credit and an exclusion, you cannot use the the same expenses to claim both.
- If the child is a citizen or resident of the United States when the adoption begins, you can take the credit or the exclusion even if the adoption never becomes final. However, if you have qualifying expenses in connection with a failed adoption attempt and later adopt another child, you must treat all qualifying expenses as one adoption effort and are therefore limited to $5,000 (or $6,000 if the child is special needs) for the tax credit.

- There is a one year delay in taking the adoption credit for domestic adoptions unless the adoption is finalized in the same year that it is initiated. For example, if you started an adoption in 1997, but it was not finalized, you could not take the tax credit for the expenses you paid in 1997 until the 1998 tax year. If your adoption was still not final in 1998, you would have to delay claiming the tax credit for your 1998 expenses until 1999.
- Expenses related to an international adoption cannot be claimed until after the adoption has been finalized.
- If your employer reimburses you for adoption expenses, you can claim the exclusion in the year the adoption becomes final or any year thereafter, if payment does not occur until later.
- You cannot take a credit for any expenses paid before 1997 or after 2001.
- Married couples must file a joint income tax return in order to qualify for the tax credit or the exclusion.
- You must provide your child's name, birth date, and Social Security number or taxpayer identification number on your return.
- Certain expenses such as home construction or renovation and vehicle alteration which are necessary to provide for a special needs child may qualify for the tax credit.
- You must continue to have taxes withheld from your paycheck even though you expect to receive a tax credit.

Carryover Provisions

- Your credit or exclusion cannot be more than your tax liability for that year minus any credits for child and dependent care expenses, the elderly or the disabled, or mortgage interest and your tentative minimum tax.

- If your tax liability is less than the amount of the credit to which you are entitled, you can carry over any remaining amount into the next five tax years or until the initial credit is used.

Financing Strategies

Employer-sponsored reimbursement programs and the adoption tax credit contribute significantly to making adoption feasible for more and more families. There are, however, still factors which make it difficult for some families. Adoptive parents must have the necessary funds to cover all expenses up-front, and then wait for reimbursement or tax refunds. The following strategies might help to secure the necessary funds:

- Obtaining a second mortgage or home equity loan
- Borrowing money from your 401K account
- Having a yard sale
- Asking your family, friends, or your church to sponsor your child
- Seeking an agency that receives charitable funds such as United Way to help reduce the costs of services
- Obtaining a grant or loan (see chapter 11 for information about organizations that assist with adoption expenses)

Chapter 4

International Adoption—an Overview

ne of the most rewarding types of adoption is perhaps international. While the path may be riddled with obstacles, the end result is a child rich in cultural history, often different from your own.

EVALUATING THE ISSUES

It is difficult to clearly define the advantages and disadvantages of any type of adoption, as each prospective parent will have a different interpretation of the issues. There are many complex factors which will influence the decision to pursue a specific type of adoption. The following is an overview of some basic assumptions with regard to international adoptions.

Advantages

Availability of children In general, there are many more children in need of families than there are families seeking to adopt. Families who are patient, persistent, and flexible are almost always successful in adopting a child internationally. Due to constantly changing laws and regulations in our country as well as others, the path one initially chooses for adoption may not work out. A moratorium on international adoptions in one country may mean that prospective parents must be open to entering an adoption program in another country. Each country has its own set of requirements so it is a good idea to look at all the programs offered by an agency or facilitator to see if you qualify for programs other than the one in which you are interested.

Relatively short process Most international adoptions take between six months and two years to complete. While this sounds like a long time for children who need families to be united with families who are eager to love them, it is really incredibly short when one takes into account all the various entities involved. Adoptive families must comply with all the requirements of their home study agency, the international agency, their state of residence, the United States of America, and the foreign country. There are many people involved in issuing documents, preparing reports, signing forms, etc. A successful adoption requires the dedication and cooperation of numerous people in both countries.

Security of final decree It is very rare that an international adoption is challenged or questioned after the child has arrived in this country. This is due in part to the fact that the authorities in the child's birth country have carefully scrutinized the paperwork prior to issuance of the passport and that the U.S. Embassy or Consulate has also taken action to determine whether the child's adoption is valid. In countries where there is believed to be a high level of fraud in the society in general or where there have been prior reports of children being kidnapped for international adoption, the U.S. officials may interview birth parents or others involved. In some situations, DNA testing may even be required to prove that a person is indeed the birth mother of a particular child. The U.N. recommends that children not be adopted from a country that is in turmoil until at least two years have passed. This allows time for parents or other relatives to find the child in the event that the family became separated during the chaos of war.

Disadvantages

Unknown background   In some cases, children have been abandoned and there is no information available about their birth parents. In other cases, background information is not available due to poor access to medical care, inadequate recordkeeping, or differing opinions about the type of information that is valuable or necessary. When a child enters the orphanage or foster care system due to a crisis situation, the preliminary goal is often family reunification. Therefore, the person who is acting as the intake worker may not ask the birth parents for all the information that might be requested if the goal is adoption for the child. Later on, when the efforts to reunite the family are not successful, it may be impossible to obtain the desired information.

It also happens occasionally that information which is known but which is perceived to be negative is not shared with prospective adoptive parents. The motivation for withholding negative information (such as a history of mental illness in the birth mother) may be based upon fear that the child's chances for adoption will be drastically reduced if potential adopters know the truth. Adoption professionals in this country overwhelmingly agree that all information, no matter how negative, is vital to the success of an adoption. However, not everyone who is in a key position to influence the gathering and distribution of information is well-educated about adoption issues and how they affect the adoptee as he/she goes through life. Imagine for a moment that you have the responsibility for helping a child move into a permanent family. Would you want to present the child in the most favorable way, pointing out his/her strengths rather than his/her weaknesses? Most people who are involved in the process truly want the child to have a happy life with a family. If you have collected all the available information about the child and sought advice from experts who are uncertain what his/her prognosis or potential is, you will have to follow your own heart in deciding whether to accept the child.

Dealing with another layer of bureaucracy   Families adopting children internationally have to go through significantly more bureaucratic red tape than those adopting domestically. They must satisfy the requirements of their state of residence, the U.S. Immigration and Naturalization Service, and the child's home country. Sorting through all the necessary requirements and making sure that they are all met can be a daunting task. It can be very stressful, especially if you choose to pursue an international adoption without the advice of an experienced agency or facilitator.

Adoption regulations may change overnight, especially in countries where international adoptions are relatively "new." There is a normal cycle that seems to happen when a country opens its doors to international adoption. At first, with only a few adoptions being completed, there is little public attention to the fact that children are leaving the country. As more and more adoptive families travel to complete their adoptions, the public awareness is heightened. Consider, for example, that the U.S. Consulate in Guangzhou, the People's Republic of China, processed over two hundred and fifty visas for adopted children each month in 1996. This means that roughly the same number of adoptive families traveled to Guangzhou and stayed in one of a dozen or more hotels. It is very difficult for that many foreigners to go unnoticed by the local residents. Inevitably, there will be factions of the society who question why the children are being allowed to leave the country, whether their rights are being protected, and whether the adopting parents have genuine motives. As politicians begin to evaluate the process and respond to allegations of abuse or fraud in the system, laws are usually revised numerous times. It is not unusual to see a moratorium placed on international adoptions until new laws can be written and implemented. When a new system is in place, it usually takes several months for everyone to fully understand it, and then things seem to settle back down. However, it is not uncommon for there to be new laws or policies introduced every year or so for the first five or ten years that a country is engaging in international adoptions.

Institutional care The majority of the countries from which children are adopted internationally have a child welfare system that includes a much higher proportion of public or private institutions than foster families or small-group homes. While there are many very good and caring facilities all over the world, children living in institutions do not get as much one-on-one attention as they do in a family setting. Therefore, almost all children living in institutions will experience developmental delays. Minor health problems such as scabies, malnutrition, anemia, and dental problems may go untreated. However, most developmental and health concerns can be easily addressed upon arrival here. Adoptive parents must be prepared to research the services available in their area and to seek any assistance their child may need.

There has been a great deal of media attention in recent years to the attachment problems suffered by children living in institutions, particularly in Eastern Europe. Children who have not received adequate stimulation and care as infants may need extra attention from their adoptive parents or from professionals to help them make up for lost time. See the chapter on resources for adoptive parents for more information about centers that specialize in evaluating medical records from other countries and treating children adopted internationally. They can also provide referrals to appropriate specialists in your area.

Advantages/Disadvantages

Lack of contact with the birth family   For some families, the decision to pursue an international adoption is a relief because it means there will be very little likelihood of ongoing contact with the child's birth family. Many people, understandably, feel anxious or intimidated by the prospect of having a birth parent involved in their adopted child's life.

In cases of abandonment or termination of parental rights due to abuse or neglect, adoptive families lose the ability to have contact, however anonymous, with the birth family. This can be a source of sadness for the child and the adoptive parents must be prepared to acknowledge the child's grief. In countries where birth parents are allowed to make an adoption plan for the child, the adoptive parents can establish a ritual of sending a letter and photographs once a year, perhaps on the child's birthday, to the agency or attorney that handled the adoption. In many cases, birth parents can remain in contact with the agency or attorney and see photographs or have nonidentifying information about the child. As the child grows up and begins to wonder whether his birth parents ever think about him, the adoptive parents can show him copies of the letters and pictures they have sent to his home country and assure him that the information will be available to them if they desire it. Even when birth parents are unknown, it is very important for adoptive families to send letters and pictures to the child welfare officials in the child's birth country on a regular basis. Pictures of happy children go a long way in promoting a good attitude toward international adoption and serve to dispel any negative rumors that may come up.

In spite of its negative connotations in our society, abandonment rarely means that the birth parents had little regard for the child. In most situations, children are abandoned in a very public place, such as a hospital, train station, or shopping center where they will be found very quickly. It is also possible in such a setting for the birth parent to remain nearby until the child is found. Because some societies do not have the legal or social service systems in place for birth parents to make adoption plans for their children, abandonment is the only alternative, even for the most loving and caring parents. It is more difficult for adoptive parents to understand and be empathetic toward birth parents who have neglected or abused their children but it is vital to the child's self-esteem that they make a genuine attempt to be nonjudgmental. It is okay to tell the child that the birth parents faced a very difficult situation and did not know where to turn and that they probably think about him or her and hope that he or she is healthy and happy.

Travel Traveling to the child's county of birth allows the adoptive parents to become acquainted with the child's culture and to develop a better understanding of where he/she has lived prior to adoption and meet his/her caretakers, etc. It also allows the parents to be with the child alone without the normal pressures of life at home and they can spend a great deal of time playing with and bonding to the child. For some, it is a disadvantage due to the inability to travel for health or financial reasons.

The trend in international adoption at this time is that most countries require adoptive parents to travel so they can appear in court and affirm their commitment to a specific child, finalize the adoption, and obtain the child's passport and visa. Some countries allow one parent to travel alone with a Power of Attorney from the other spouse. Finalizing the adoption overseas with the adoptive parents present allows the foreign government to insure that the child is a permanent legal member of his adoptive family.

Visibility   Families who adopt children internationally often become more visible to society at large because their members do not look like one another. For some, diversity is welcome, and for others it can be unsettling to experience the stares of strangers. Adoptive parents need to be prepared to handle insensitive questions or comments with tact.

The Process

Even though actual procedures and paperwork will vary from one country to another as well as from one agency to another, there are basic elements that will be common to all international adoptions. It is helpful for prospective parents to have a general understanding of these elements when they begin researching international adoption. The following framework will give you some idea of what needs to happen in order for a successful adoption to take place and will also help you to formulate some questions for agencies or facilitators as you make your decisions.

The Child

Identity   A child's identity must be established through an official birth record in his/her country of birth. In cases of true abandonment, where the actual date of birth or identity of birth parents are not known, there will be an estimated date of birth.

For children who are very young (a few months old) at the time they enter the child welfare system, there is usually very little room for error in estimating a birth date. For children who are beyond infancy, there can be a great deal of error. Some parents report finding out later, through bone x-rays or other medical tests, that their children were as much as two years older or younger than their birth record indicated. In many cases, the officials in the child's country will evaluate the child's intellectual and emotional development as well as his/her physical development in assigning a presumed date of birth. These measures may be unreliable due to poor nutrition, lack of intellectual or physical stimulation, or a history of medical problems which make the child appear younger than he/she is.

Termination of parental rights   The rights of the child's birth parents must be terminated. When the birth parents are known and make a voluntary adoption plan for the child, they may be required to simply sign an affidavit in front of an attorney or notary public or they may be required to appear in court. If the whereabouts of one of the birth parents is unknown, a search may be conducted. The exact means taken to locate the birth parent must be documented and the results of the search given. In some countries, this will involve placing an advertisement in the local newspaper regarding the child's abandonment and/or pending adoption case. It may also involve interviewing past employers, neighbors, or relatives of the birth parent, if such information is available. If a birth parent is deceased, a copy of the death certificate will be required.

When children are abandoned, there will also be a search for the birth parents as required by the laws of the child's country. The search may include interviewing the staff at the hospital where the child was found, for example. One relatively common way in which children are abandoned is for the birth mother to enter the hospital under an assumed name and then leave during the night without the baby. When the officials go to look for her, they may find that the address she gave to the hospital is that of a vacant lot. In all countries, there is a procedure which must be followed to ensure that efforts have been made to locate the birth parents of the child. If the child's birth parents are not found, the child can then be declared legally abandoned.

When children are removed from the birth parents due to neglect or abuse, there may have been some efforts made to reunite the family. The length of time spent on rehabilitation or reunification measures will be determined by the prevailing laws and standards of practice in that country.

It is not uncommon that children are taken to children's homes or orphanages by their birth parents and left with the promise that the parents will return when they get a job, a place to live, receive medical treatment, etc. If the birth parents do not return, the process for having the child declared abandoned will be initiated. The length of time that must pass before it is determined unlikely that the birth parents will return varies from as little as a few months to several years.

Eligibility for international adoption Once the rights of the birth parents are terminated, the child must be deemed eligible for international adoption. In some countries, such as Russia and Romania, there are local and/or national registries where information about children in need of families must be made available to local citizens before international adoption can be considered. The laws of the country will dictate how long the child must remain on the registry, usually three to six months. If a prospective adoptive family in the child's home country expresses an interest in him while he is on the registry, preference will be given to them over a foreign family. If there are no local families interested in adopting the child after the required period of time has passed, the child then can be offered in international adoption. Other countries do not have systems which are as formally defined but may have a mandate that a child remain in the orphanage or foster care for a certain number of months before an international adoption can be initiated, just to allow time for his/her birth family to return to claim him. There are a few countries, for example, Guatemala, which have no formal requirements for making children available to local families first.

Eligibility for immigration   Adoptive children coming into the United States are granted visas under the Immigration and Nationality Act (INA). In order to obtain a visa, the child must be an orphan as defined in the law. The interpretation of the law may differ from one U.S. Consulate to another, even though it is a federal regulation and should be uniformly applied by all offices. Under the strictest interpretation, children who have two living parents are not eligible to emigrate to the United States unless they have been unconditionally abandoned for at least two years.

The Family

Adoptive home study evaluation   The adoptive home study is the tool through which families are evaluated for their suitability to adopt. The content and format of the home study will be determined by the laws of the state in which the adoptive parents live as well as applicable federal regulations. A more thorough discussion of the home study is found in chapter 2. A few countries will accept the adoptive home study at face value, especially in cases where the child is coming to the United States for adoption and temporary guardianship will be held by a licensed agency. The child welfare system in South Korea allows for agencies in that country to transfer guardianship directly to agencies here who can then supervise the placement for six months or more before allowing finalization of the adoption. In most countries, however, prospective adoptive families must present supporting documents as evidence of their suitability to adopt. In order to meet the requirements of the U.S. Immigration and Naturalization Service, each family must have a home study prepared by a licensed child-placing agency or adoption professional, depending upon the laws of their state of residence.

Dossier   According to Webster, a dossier is "a group of documents on the same subject, especially a complete group containing detailed information." For adoptive families, preparing the dossier can be the most overwhelming phase of the whole process. The dossier requirements will vary from one country to another and even from one agency to another working in the same country. Examples of items that might be included in the dossier are:

- Birth certificates
- Marriage certificate
- Divorce decrees or death certificates of former spouses
- Medical reports
- Police clearances
- Employment certificates
- Proof of property ownership
- Letters of recommendation
- Psychological or psychiatric reports

- Adoptive home study
- Power of attorney for the person who will represent the family in the child's country
- Photographs of the family and their home
- Notice of INS approval (form I-171H)

The purpose of these documents is to provide firsthand information in support of the adoptive family's petition or application to adopt. All the information should be consistent throughout the dossier; for example, the income reported in the home study should match the amount stated in the employment letters. A more detailed description of the preparation of the dossier can be found later in this chapter.

Approval of the adoptive family   All countries have a system through which adoptive families are approved prior to placement of a child. In some countries, it is a formal process conducted by a specific office of the central government. In others, it is conducted by the licensed child welfare agencies or by the courts. There are often several entities involved in the adoption process and it may include representatives from the education, welfare, civil affairs, and/or justice divisions of the local government.

The Adoption

Making the connection   The term "matching" is sometimes used to the describe the process by which a child is offered or assigned to a specific family for adoption. This term is somewhat antiquated in that it implies that children and families will be united based upon shared characteristics. In international adoptions, children are often of a different racial and ethnic background than their adoptive families.

The criteria used to determine which family can best meet a child's needs are more often based upon the family's stated preferences and abilities and the child's age, sex, and mental and physical condition. Child assignment may be done by the officials in his home country. In the People's Republic of China, for example, the China Centre for Adoption Affairs approves the family for adoption and selects the child to be placed with them. The family then has the option to decline acceptance of the child based upon the medical and social information provided. In other countries, the U.S. agency handling the adoption has the authority to select a family for a child, subject to final approval by the overseas officials. In countries that allow independent adoptions, the adoptive family may locate a child to adopt through the use of an intermediary such as a relative, friend, attorney, missionary, or social worker.

Transfer of guardianship After an adoptive family has accepted a child for placement in their home, a transfer of guardianship or a final adoption can be initiated. Legal responsibility for the child must be transferred to a licensed child-placing agency or the adoptive parents before he/she can leave the country. This process may be handled by the courts or by other government agencies. It will involve a review of the dossier submitted by the adoptive family, a review of the documents prepared on behalf of the child (birth certificate, surrender or termination of parental rights, death certificates of parents, etc.), and in most countries, a personal interview with one or both of the adoptive parents. Agency representatives or facilitators in the child's home country can often handle many of the initial steps in this process before the adoptive family arrives. In some countries, there is a waiting period after the adoption hearing during which objections to the finalization of the adoption can be filed and adoptive parents may be required to remain in the country until the waiting period has passed. In other cases, two trips may be necessary, one to initiate the adoption proceedings and the second to finalize the adoption and obtain the child's U.S. Immigrant visa.

Establishing the child's identity In cases where the adoption is finalized in the child's home country, a new or amended birth certificate will be issued. The new certificate will include the names of the adoptive parents and perhaps the date of the adoption. All children, regardless of whether or not the adoption has been finalized, will need a passport to travel to the United States.

Issuance of the immigrant visa Children coming to live permanently in the United States must obtain an immigrant visa at the American Consulate or Embassy that serves their home country. A detailed description of the process can be found later in this chapter.

The Dossier

Compiling and preparing a dossier is a very time-consuming task which requires attention to detail and a great deal of organization. Some agencies assist adoptive families in the process of gathering documents and having them appropriately legalized, others offer advice and suggestions to help the applicants prepare the dossier on their own. Adoptive parents may also choose to use the services of a dossier preparation service or seek advice from other members of their adoptive parent support group who have recently adopted internationally. The ability to prioritize matters and focus attention on those documents that will take longer to obtain is essential. The complexity of preparing the dossier will depend upon the country in which you are adopting as well as the number of states in which your documents originate. Each foreign country has their own requirements for the format of the documents and, unfortunately, each Secretary of State in this country has its own requirements for the format of the documents. It helps to do a lot of research before you begin collecting the documents.

A few countries accept dossier documents which have been notarized only. Most countries, however, require that dossier documents be legalized. Legalization is a means of verifying that the individuals whose names appear on the documents are authorized to act in their stated capacities. There are two types of legalization: apostille certification and authentication. In most cases, apostille certification is less complicated than authentication. The Hague Convention of October 5, 1961 allows for apostille certification of documents by the Secretary of State or its designee and simplifies the flow of documents among party nations. Mexico and Russia, for example, are two of the member nations; therefore documents can be apostille certified in the state(s) where they originate and sent overseas without further attachments. Authentication involves obtaining the seal of the foreign government on each document through its Consulate or Embassy in this country. Most countries require that documents first be certified (this is different than apostille certification) by the Secretary of State prior to being presented for authentication. The foreign Embassies and Consulates have jurisdiction for certain geographical areas of the United States, so documents must be sent to the office that serves the state(s) where they originate. Adoptive parents who live in the states served by the Embassy of a given country must first send their documents to the U.S. Department of State for authentication prior to sending them to the Embassy.

There are two types of documents which will be included in the dossier: official records and notarized documents. Official records such as birth, marriage, and divorce certificates must be originals issued by the authorities entrusted with keeping such records. All official records which are to be apostille certified must meet the guidelines set forth by the Secretary of State. Official records which are to be authenticated may or may not require the seal of the Secretary of State, depending upon the country in which they are to be used. Many Secretaries of State will only certify (apostille or other) the document if it has an original signature. It is helpful to know whether an original signature is needed when ordering official records, since certified copies usually only have a facsimile signature and a raised seal. Documents which have been notarized must be certified by the Secretary of State in the state in which they originated in all cases. In some states (Alabama, Georgia, Kentucky, Maryland, New York, Ohio, Oklahoma, and Tennessee), certification of the notary or local official is required at the county level first before the document can be certified by the Secretary of State.

Once the dossier documents have been gathered and appropriately legalized, they must be translated. In some cases, translations can be done here in the United States by a qualified translator. In other cases, translations must be prepared by official translators in the country where the adoption is to be completed. It is very important for adoptive parents to keep in mind when they are gathering their documents that simplicity is the key to good translations. Letters or reports which contain complicated phrases can easily be misunderstood when translated into another language by someone who is not familiar with our culture. It is also possible that phrases or words that seem very clear to a native English speaker can be misinterpreted. I once worked with an adoptive father who had been a conscientious objector during the Vietnam war. In the home study I wrote that he had "served" as an orderly in a hospital for two years during the war. When the home study was translated into Spanish overseas, the word that was used for "served" meant "imprisoned." Then, the officials questioned why his police certificate stated that he had no criminal record when he had been imprisoned for two years. Fortunately, the attorney was able to explain the misunderstanding and the adoption was completed. Situations like this one illustrate the importance of having a good advocate in the foreign country, whether it is an attorney, a facilitator, or an agency representative.

IMMIGRATION
The Visa

As with the adoption process itself, the immigration process has components that pertain to the adoptive family and those that pertain to the child. In most cases, adoptive families do not already know about a specific child whom they would like to adopt when they begin the immigration process. There is a lot of preliminary work that can be done for the family to be approved for international adoption prior to locating a child. It is advisable to initiate this part of the process as early as possible since it can take several months, depending upon where you live. At least one of the prospective adoptive parents must be a U.S. citizen to complete the immigration process described here.

All families will be required to file form I-600 (Petition to Classify Orphan as an Immediate Relative) at some point. However, that form requires information about the child to be adopted and supporting documents. If a child has not already been identified, prospective parents can file form I-600A (Application for Advance Processing of Orphan Petition) with their local Immigration and Naturalization Service (INS) office. To obtain these forms, call 1-800-870-3676 or order them online at http://www.ins.usdoj.gov/exec/forms. In support of the I-600A application, the following documents will be needed:

- proof of U.S. citizenship (copies of birth and/or naturalization records)
- proof of current marriage
- proof of termination of all prior marriages
- fingerprint cards for all adult members of the household
- adoptive home study

All items except the home study may be submitted prior to completion of the home study to expedite processing of the file. The fee for filing the petition is $155 at the time of this writing and must be paid by money order or certified check in U.S. funds. A proposed fee increase is being considered which would make the fee for filing this form $405. As of March 30, 1998, fingerprints for all adult members of the household must be prepared by an INS service office, an INS approved law enforcement agency, or an Application Support Center (ASC). After filing form I-600 or I-600A, the applicants will receive a letter from INS notifying them of the week in which they should appear to have their fingerprints taken. If they cannot go that week, they can appear on any Wednesday for a period of eighty-four days following the date of the week they are originally scheduled for fingerprinting. The fingerprinting fee is $25 per adult and must be paid with a certified check or money order. The fingerprints will be sent to the FBI for a criminal record search and upon receipt of a favorable report from the FBI and an approved adoptive home study, the applicant will be notified of approval of the application (form I-171H). The approval is valid for eighteen months from the date of approval of advance processing which is found in the box at the upper right hand corner of the document. In many states, the home study must be submitted to INS by the state's Division of Social Services with a letter stating that the preadoption requirements have been met. If the applicants will be traveling to the child's country, a Visas 37 cable will be sent to the U.S. Consulate or Embassy which serves that country. In an effort to centralize services, some U.S. Consulates serve several countries and adoptive parents may need to travel to a country other than that of their child's birth to obtain the visa. For example, visas for children born in Vietnam are processed at the U.S. Consulate in Bangkok, Thailand.

You can file form I-600A even before you have decided upon a country and an agency. If you are uncertain where you plan to adopt, you can ask for your file to be held at the local service office until further notification. At any point prior to completion of your home study and approval of your I-600A petition, you can notify INS in writing about where you plan to adopt and whether you would like your file to be forwarded overseas. If you don't make a final decision until after your I-171H form has been issued or if you subsequently decide to adopt a child from a country other than the one you originally indicated, you can file form I-824 (Application for Action on an Approved Application or Petition) to request that an approval cable be sent to the appropriate Consulate.

In many countries, form I-171H is part of the dossier and the foreign officials will not consider your application to adopt a child until they know that you have been approved by the U.S. government. This is the main reason for filing the forms early. Another reason is that you cannot bring your child into the United States until I-171H has been issued. Thus, even if you travel overseas and complete an adoption, the U.S. Consulate will not grant a visa to your child without notification of approval from your local INS office.

After a child has been identified, the parents can file form I-600 with their local service office or with the U.S. consular office abroad, depending upon whether they will be traveling. The following documents will be required in support of form I-600:

- proof of U. S. citizenship (copies of birth and/or naturalization records)
- proof of current marriage
- proof of termination of all prior marriages
- fingerprint cards for all adult members of the household—these are not filed with the form, but are scheduled by INS after form I-600A is filed
- adoptive home study (must be less than six months old)
- proof of age of orphan
- death certificate of the child's parent(s), if applicable
- certified copy of the adoption decree or guardianship order along with a certified translation
- evidence that the child has been unconditionally abandoned to an orphanage or his/her sole or surviving parent has in writing irrevocably released him/her for emigration and adoption

It is, of course, unnecessary to file additional copies of documents which were filed with form I-600A. If all the documents pertaining to the child or the home study are not ready at the time of filing, they can be submitted within one year.

There are two types of immigrant visas issued to children who have been or will be adopted by U.S. citizens. The IR-3 visa is issued when the adoption has been completed overseas AFTER the child has been personally seen by both spouses or by the single adoptive parent. The IR-4 visa is issued when the child has been adopted overseas without having been personally seen by the adoptive parents or when the child is coming to the United States for adoption. Children who receive an IR-3 visa are immediately eligible to apply for U.S. citizenship upon arrival in this country. Children who receive an IR-4 visa cannot apply for citizenship until the adoption has been finalized in their state of residence.

In some cases, adoptive families must travel overseas to meet their child prior to finalization of the adoption even if the foreign government does not require their presence. There are a few states that do not allow domestication of a foreign decree. If you live in one of those states and you are adopting a child from a country where the adoption is finalized abroad by proxy, such as in Guatemala, you will need to see the child prior to finalization in order to apply for U.S. citizenship for him or her.

When the adoption or guardianship process has been completed, the adoptive parents or their representative must arrange for a visa interview at the appropriate U.S. Consulate. The requirements for the visa interview may vary slightly from one consular office to another so it is always a good idea to make sure that you or your representative know the specific requirements. In many cases, adoptive families will receive an information packet from the U.S. consular office outlining the procedures to be followed after their I-171H has been received. In all cases, the child must be personally seen by a consular officer prior to issuance of the visa. The following documentation will be required:

- notification of approval of form I-600 or I-600A
- the child's birth certificate
- adoption decree or guardianship order
- photographs of the child
- form OF230 (visa application)
- form I-600 if not previously approved
- form I-604 (Request for Report on Overseas Orphan Investigation)
- form 157 (Medical Examination of Applicants for U.S. visas)—this form must be completed by a panel physical approved by the U.S. Consulate after the issuance of your child's passport

- form I-864 (Affidavit of Support)—this form has been in use since December 19, 1997 and requires extensive documentation of your financial situation (letters from employers, copies of your last three years of 1040 tax returns, etc.)

All the required forms can be obtained from the U.S. Consulate where the visa will be issued. When all of the above have been submitted, the U.S. Consular officer will review everything to make sure that the preadoption requirements of the child's proposed state of residence have been met, that the child is an orphan, that the legal requirements for transfer of guardianship have been satisfied, that he/she is free from contagious diseases, and that he/she has the appropriate travel documentation. The fee for the visa application is now $260 and the fee for issuance is $65 ($325 total). After the final visa interview has been completed and a favorable determination has been made, the child's visa is usually issued in twenty-four to forty-eight hours. The child is now ready to travel. However, final authority for permission to enter the United States rests with the INS officials at the child's port of entry.

Residency

A child admitted to the United States on an IR-3 or IR-4 visa will be a permanent legal resident of this country. Upon arrival in the United States, the INS officer who admits the child will stamp his/her passport to reflect the type of visa he/she has and the file number under which his/her records will be kept. At the bottom of the stamp will be a date, usually six months from the date of entry. The child should receive his/her Alien Registration card sometime prior to the date under the stamp. If you do not receive the card close to that date, call the INS at 1-800-375-5283. The Alien Registration card is also known as the "green card" even though they are no longer green. The card itself is laminated and looks very similar to a driver's license. It has a small photograph of the child on a pink and cream background. This card will serve as proof of the child's permanent resident status until he/she obtains U.S. citizenship and should be carried with him/her at all times.

Every permanent resident is entitled to a Social Security number. Adoptive parents must apply with their local Social Security office as soon as possible after their child arrives. If the adoption has not been completed overseas or if the final adoption order did not include a name change for the child, the Social Security card will be issued in the name that appears on the child's passport, which may not be the name that the adoptive parents have chosen. After the adoption is completed in the family's state of residence, a request for a name change can be filed with the Social Security Administration. The procedure is similar to that which is followed when women file for a new card in their married name. The Social Security records should also be amended when the child becomes a U.S. citizen.

Citizenship

After the adoptive family has finally succeeded in locating a child and bringing him/her to this country, it is easy for them to be so overwhelmed with their new responsibilities that they procrastinate on obtaining citizenship. It is very important, however, that this final step of the process be completed. Adopted children who do not become U.S. citizens may be subject to deportation if they commit a crime as teenagers or adults.

If a child has entered this country on an IR-3 visa, the application for citizenship can be made immediately. If he/she has entered on an

IR-4 visa, the adoption must be finalized in his/her state of residence prior to filing the application. If both of the adoptive parents are U.S. citizens, they should file form N-643 (Application for Certificate of Citizenship in Behalf of an Adopted Child) with their local INS office. The filing fee is $80 at the time of this writing and is proposed to increase to $125. The form can be ordered at 1-800-8870-3676. In support of this application, the following items will be needed:

- child's Alien Registration card
- child's birth certificate
- final adoption decree
- three identical passport-sized photographs of the child
- proof of U.S. citizenship for adoptive parents
- proof of marriage
- proof of termination of all prior marriages

In order to use form N-643, both adoptive parents must be U.S. citizens. If either of the parents is not a U.S. citizen, form N-400 (Application for Naturalization) must be used. Processing time for either form takes about six to nine months and adoptive parents will be notified of the date and time for the interview. If the child is obtaining a Certificate of Citizenship, the certificate will either be issued at the time of the interview or mailed to the family shortly afterward. If the child is obtaining a Certificate of Naturalization, the family will be notified of the date of the Naturalization ceremony at which time the child will receive the certificate. Each INS service office handles these ceremonies differently. Some have a special ceremony just for adopted children and others have a ceremony that includes adults as well as children. Most INS offices prefer that adoptive families use form N-643 whenever possible.

The Future of International Adoptions— The Hague Convention

In 1994, the United States signed the Hague Convention on Protection of Children and Co-operation in Respect of Intercountry Adoption. This a multilateral treaty adopted by the Hague Conference on Private International Law in May 29, 1993, after several years of negotiations among the member nations. The next step is for the United States to ratify the treaty, which will require federal legislation aimed at ensuring uniform implementation of Convention requirements around the country. Proposed legislation is presently being consider by the Office of Management and Budget (OMB). It is expected that ratification will occur in the next two to three years.

The Hague Convention will affect the future of international adoptions within the United States regardless of whether or not we ratify it. It is designed to create a formal system among party nations that will protect the rights of children and allow for closer monitoring of intercountry adoption activities. Countries that are parties to the Hague Convention will probably be reluctant to allow children to be adopted into countries that are not parties.

Each party nation shall establish a Central Authority to oversee the implementation of the treaty and cooperate with and provide information to Central Authorities in other party nations. The Central Authority shall also handle all complaints with regard to intercountry adoption. It may delegate certain functions to other public organizations or formally accredited agencies.

The "sending" nation must ensure that the child is adoptable, that an intercountry adoption is in his/her best interests, and that the birth parents have voluntarily relinquished their rights to him/her after appropriate counseling. The "receiving" nation must establish that the prospective parents are eligible to adopt, that they have received counseling about the adoption process, and that the child is able to enter and reside permanently in their country.

The Hague Convention is an exciting development because it is the first time that there has been an official intergovernmental approval of international adoption. In the past, many nations have viewed international adoption as a last resort for children who could not be adequately cared for in their own country (including institutional care). This treaty acknowledges that a child needs to grow up in a family filled with love, happiness, and understanding in order to develop to his or her full potential. It also recognizes the need for adoption counseling and postadoption services and encourages the Central Authorities to develop training programs for adoption professionals. It will also mean added security for the child and the adoptive family with regard to the validity of the adoption. One possible added benefit is that the citizenship process may be simplified for children adopted under the Convention and they may be able to travel on U.S. passports rather than on immigrant visas.

Chapter 5

International Adoption—Choosing a Country

*N*ow that you've chosen to give international adoption a try, it's time for the next major decision: choosing a country. You may want a child with a simular ethnic heritage as your own, or you may end up with a beautiful child from a country about which you know very little! Once a country is chosen, however, there is often a long wait ahead—time well-spent learning everything you can about your future child's homeland.

WHERE ARE THE CHILDREN?

Each year, thousands of children from around the world are adopted by U.S. citizens. The following chart shows statistics based upon the number of immigrant visas issued to adopted children, by country of origin. Some countries have been involved in international adoption for many years and have a relatively stable number of adoptions. Others, Russia and China, for example, have been developing their international adoption system only in recent years. Changing political climates have dramatically affected the number of children being adopted internationally in any given country.

Country	FY '89	FY '90	FY '91	FY '92	FY '93	FY '94	FY '95	FY '96
Bolivia	27	30	46	73	124	37	21	33
Brazil	175	228	175	138	161	149	146	103
Bulgaria	1	3	9	91	133	97	110	163
Cambodia	0	15	60	15	1	3	10	32
Chile	253	302	266	179	61	79	90	63
China	201	29	61	206	330	787	2,130	3,333
Colombia	736	631	521	404	426	351	350	255
Costa Rica	78	105	56	64	48	29	19	20
Cuba	95	0	19	0	0	0	0	
Dominican Republic	68	58	50	42	39	17	15	13
Ecuador	20	59	10	37	49	48	67	51
El Salvador	94	103	123	117	100	38	306	17
Ethiopia	6	18	15	37	30	54	63	44
Georgia	0	0	0	2	3	17	51	77
Guatemala	202	257	329	418	512	436	449	427
Haiti	80	64	49	16	51	61	49	68
Honduras	181	197	234	249	179	77	28	28
Hong Kong	54	36	49	29	30	34	30	

India	648	348	445	352	331	412	371	380
Jamaica	42	28	41	27	48	35	45	34
Japan	74	57	87	68	64	49	63	36
Korea	3,544	2,620	1,818	1,840	1,775	1,795	1,666	1,516
Latvia	0	0	0	4	15	33	59	77
Lithuania	0	0	0	0	24	95	98	73
Mexico	91	112	97	91	91	85	83	76
Paraguay	252	282	190	212	412	483	351	258
Peru	222	440	705	309	224	37	15	17
Philippines	465	421	393	357	360	314	298	229
Poland	74	66	92	109	70	94	30	62
Romania	138	121	2,594	121	97	199	275	555
Russia	0	0	0	324	746	1,530	1,896	2,454
Taiwan	75	66	54	36	32	35	23	19
Thailand	109	100	131	86	69	47	53	55
Ukraine	0	0	0	55	273	164	4	1
Vietnam	15	52	37	22	110	220	318	354
World Total	8,102	7,093	9,050	6,472	7,377	8,333	9,679	11,340

(FY refers to Fiscal Year. This information was obtained from the U.S. Department of State, Bureau of Consular Affairs.)

REQUIREMENTS

Requirements in each country change continuously and the only reliable way to know the current situation at any given time is to consult with an agency, facilitator, or other adoption professional who is actively involved in adoptions. The U.S. Department of State, through the Office of Children's Issues, can provide general information about adoptions in various countries. The phone number is (202) 647-2688. Their website is http://travel.state.gov/children's_issues.html. There are also several organizations which offer publications about international adoptions and country requirements as well as lists of agencies. See the chapter on resources for further information.

The requirements in effect at this time in Russia, the People's Republic of China, and Korea are presented for illustration only:

According to Mercy Reed Marchuk of Maine Adoption Placement Service (MAPS), the responsibility for caring for children in Russia is handled by the Ministry of Education. Children who cannot live with their birth families for whatever reason, reside in public children's homes. Each region of the country has its own child-caring institutions and children under the age of three are usually housed separately from children over three. The Ministry of Education officials in each region submit social and medical information on adoptable children under their care to the central office in Moscow. The information is then entered into the databank and is made available to Russian families seeking to adopt. After at least three months have passed, if the child has not been adopted, the local officials can send an inquiry to Moscow for permission to offer the child in international adoption. After confirmation from Moscow that the child can be adopted by a foreign family, the regional officials or children's home directors can seek the assistance of adoption agencies or facilitators to locate a family.

Adoptive parents should be of an "appropriate" age to adopt a given child. The law is not specific about exact age requirements, marital status, length of marriage, or prior divorces. MAPS and many other agencies use forty-five years as a maximum age difference between the parents and the child they can petition to adopt. Final approval for the adoption is dependent upon the local courts in the region where the child lives as well as the Ministry of Education officials. The Russian child welfare system operates similarly to ours in many ways because the regional officials have flexibility in setting requirements just the same as our state officials do. Travel is required for one or both parents for one to two weeks.

In the People's Republic of China, responsibility for the care of orphaned or abandoned children is held by the Ministry of Civil Affairs, Department of Social Welfare. There is no existing social system in place to allow birth parents to relinquish children for adoption or to arrange for temporary care outside the family. Therefore, children whose parents cannot care for them are sometimes abandoned. When a child is abandoned, he/she is taken to a local children's home and a search is conducted for the parents, which may include advertisements in the newspaper. If a parent cannot be found after two months, the child is declared abandoned and is adoptable. Chinese families seeking to adopt a child can go to the children's home and inquire about children who are in need of homes. The provincial officials who are in charge of the local children's homes submit medical and social information about the children in their care to the China Centre for Adoption Affairs (CCAA) in Beijing. The CCAA is another division of the Ministry of Civil Affairs which is responsible for approving foreign families for adoption and assigning children. Chinese law requires that parents seeking to adopt healthy children must be at least thirty-five years old and childless. Parents younger than thirty-five or who already have children (through birth or adoption) may be considered for the adoption of children with special needs. There are no restrictions with regard to length of marriage or number of previous marriages. Single applicants are accepted. Household incomes must be at least $10,000 per family member annually. Adoptive parents must travel to the People's Republic of China to complete the adoption before officials from the Ministry of Justice and the Ministry of Civil Affairs. The length of stay is about two weeks.

In the Republic of South Korea, international adoption is handled by one of four adoption agencies licensed by the government. Those four agencies contract with agencies in this country and others to find homes for children who are in need of adoption. Children may be voluntarily relinquished by their birth parents. Many children live in foster homes while they are awaiting adoption. The adoption agencies in this country are required to work only with families in the states where they are licensed. However, in some cases, they are allowed to place children in other states when there is a responsible agency that agrees to work under their supervision. Under the Model Adoption Law, adoptive parents must be between twenty-five and forty-five years old. Couples should be married for at least three years. Singles are not usually accepted. Adoptive parents are not required to travel to Korea and children may be escorted to their new homes. Guardianship of children is held by the adoption agency that arranged the placement for a minimum of six months, during which time postplacement reports are submitted on a regular basis. Agency consent is required for finalization to occur in the family's state of residence. After finalization, the agency must continue to supervise the placement until the child becomes a U.S. citizen.

Keep in mind that requirements may change dramatically overnight and that neither agencies here nor our government can interfere with the rights of other countries to make decisions about their children. Influencing the lives of children through adoption is a tremendous responsibility and is carried out by different governments in different ways. It is also important to carefully evaluate information provided by agencies or other organizations and sort out where there is flexibility with regard to requirements. In countries where there are national adoption laws, like Korea, there is very little room for flexibility with regard to the age of the parents. In countries where the laws are a little more vague and are dependent upon interpretation by local officials, there will be variation among agencies with regard to requirements. If you have a special situation such as a medical condition, an arrest record or numerous prior marriages, it is always a good idea to discuss your situation with someone prior to beginning the adoption process.

CHOOSING AN AGENCY

When choosing an agency to assist with an international adoption, there are some areas that need to be evaluated.

Things to Look For

Agency focus Agencies involved in international adoption must invest a significant amount of their resources into maintaining their overseas staff and/or contacts with foreign child welfare officials. Some agencies focus all their attention on adoptions and others are involved in activities other than international adoption, such as foster care, education for homeless children, maternity home care, and family preservation programs. The philosophies of such agencies are based upon the belief that it is their responsibility to help all children, not just those who will be adopted internationally. These programs generally are well-received and serve to improve the reputation of the agency and solidify the relationship with foreign officials. It is important for adoptive families to feel good about the work that their agency does and that they are genuinely working toward creating a better future for children.

Reputation   All adoption agencies are licensed in the states in which they have offices. In some states, facilitators are also licensed. The licensing authorities will provide information about the agency to the public about previous complaints, lawsuits, compliance with state regulations, etc. It is wise for any adoptive family to contact the licensing authority as well as the Attorney General and the Better Business Bureau in the state in which the agency is licensed. Negative reports should be evaluated for their relevancy to your situation.

Agencies should be prepared to provide references from other families who have worked with them in the past. Contact the references and get a feel for their experiences with the agency. Important things to ask are:

- "Did you feel that the agency was honest in its dealings with you?"
- "Were you told about potential problems in a timely manner?"
- "Did the agency give you accurate information about fees both here and overseas?"
- "Were your phone calls handled in a polite and caring manner?"
- "Were your calls returned promptly?"
- "Were the foreign staff sensitive to your needs?"
- "Did agency staff (both here and abroad) know about the current requirements and handle the paperwork efficiently?"
- "How did the foreign staff relate to the U.S. consular office staff?"

It has always been of great interest to me to sit in the U.S. Consulate and watch attorneys and adoption facilitators come and go and see how they are treated. Even though the Consulate workers are not allowed to make recommendations to the public about adoption professionals, you can learn a lot about someone's reputation just by the way that others interact with them. Of course, many times adoptive parents are so exhausted by the time they finally get to the Consulate, usually after a week or more in the foreign country, they only care about getting their child's visa and going home and are too tired to notice anything other than a really serious problem.

It is helpful to remember that the agency does not have control over the adoption process itself but does have the ethical responsibility to stay informed about changes overseas that can affect its programs and to pass that information along to families as efficiently as possible. Some agencies have newsletters that they send to families on a monthly basis. Most agencies write letters to their families when important changes occur and news needs to be spread quickly. Agencies should always be willing to explain their programs to adoptive families and help them consider other options, if necessary.

You can also check with adoptive family support groups in the state where the agency is located for references. Carefully evaluate the comments you hear, as not everyone's experience will be the same.

Location   Some families prefer to use an agency that is close to their home so that they can develop a personal relationship with the people who will be handling their case. Communicating with someone long distance about something as important as an adoption can be difficult and frustrating. Many people find it easier to build rapport with someone through face to face contacts and feel more comfortable working with an agency they "know." However, due to the tremendous resources that are needed to maintain a successful international adoption program, the trend in this country seems to be for large agencies to handle the overseas portion and local agencies to handle the home studies and postplacement. This often leaves adoptive parents with the dilemma of using a local agency with limited resources and/or experience or using a larger agency in another state. Either choice can be equally acceptable, as long as the person feels that they are being kept informed and that their concerns are being heard.

Size Agencies vary greatly in their size and number of programs offered to adoptive families. Larger agencies often have more staff and therefore more flexibility in meeting the needs of families. If someone is away from the office, there are others who can provide reliable answers to questions and make sure that document processing continues. In smaller agencies, services may be more personal but there may be delays due simply to limited staff availability.

Large agencies often have programs in several countries. If one country changes its laws, or closes or suspends international adoptions, you may decide to pursue the adoption of a child from another country without having to change agencies. In small agencies with only one or two programs, you may need to switch agencies if a program closes. Since each country has their own requirements, it is important to look at requirements for all the different programs offered by an agency to make sure that you will qualify for another program if the one in which you are interested closes unexpectedly.

Fees For many, financial issues will be a major concern and may influence the choice of an agency. Keep in mind that lower fees can sometimes mean less services. Be careful to ask questions about the way an agency handles its overseas program (do they have staff that live there, work with a facilitator, etc.) and explore the services available (postadoption counseling, etc.) even if you don't think you will need them. Adoption is a very important decision and should not be made solely on the bottom line. Compare agency services to medical care. Few people would choose to go to an inexperienced physician for major surgery or life-altering medical care just to save money. An adoption agency is only as good as the quality of its staff and the ethics of the people entrusted with handling your case. Always beware of agencies that require you to pay most of the fees before a child is offered to you for placement.

QUESTIONS TO ASK
Country-specific Questions

The family

- What are the age requirements for parents?
- Is there a minimum length of marriage?
- Are there restrictions with regard to the number of previous marriages?
- Are singles accepted?
- Are there restrictions with regard to the number of children in the home?

The child

- How do children enter the international adoption system?
- What type of care is available for children who are awaiting adoption?
- What are the ages of most of the children for whom adoptive homes are needed?

- What is the quality and availability of medical care for children?
- How reliable is the medical and social information received?
- Can adoptive parents request a child of a certain sex, age, ethnic background, or religion

The process

- Who has the responsibility for relaying information about the child to the parents?
- Who makes the decision to offer an individual child to a specific family?
- How long does it take to receive a child offer after entering the program?
- Can a family be considered for a child prior to completion of the home study and/or the INS approval?
- Is a dossier required?

- Do you provide assistance with gathering the appropriate documents and/or having them certified and authenticated?
- Is the adoption completed overseas?
- Is travel required for one or both parents?
- If travel is not required, how are escort arrangements made and how long does it normally take?

The agency

- What are the qualifications of the agency staff?
- Will your case be handled by one person or will different people help you at different stages of the process?
- Do agency staff members travel overseas? How often?
- Does the agency employ its own staff overseas or use facilitators?

- Are pre- or postadoption meetings offered that provide education and support to families?
- Does the agency have programs overseas other than adoption?

All agencies should be willing to answer any of the above questions prior to receiving an application or fees from the adoptive family. If the answers seem to be "too good to be true," they may be. Check with several different agencies with programs in the same countries and compare the answers. If one agency is promising a significantly shorter waiting time or significantly lower fees, ask for references who have recently completed adoptions and find out if the information is reliable. Talking to other adoptive parents is one of the most useful means of evaluating an agency's programs. Don't be afraid to ask for explanations of various procedures and requirements. Reputable agencies should be willing to explain the difference between agency requirements and country requirements.

Chapter 6

Domestic Adoptions—
Important Concepts

The adoption system in the United States, although relatively stable, has undergone many significant changes in the past few decades. Most of these changes have been aimed at greater protection for the rights of children. It is essential for adoptive parents to educate themselves about legal and social issues which might affect them through contact with adoption professionals and other adoptive families. The purpose of this chapter is to present some concepts with which you should be familiar and give you ideas about questions to ask.

TERMINATION OF PARENTAL RIGHTS

Before any child can be adopted, there must be a legal termination of the rights of his/her parents. In cases of abandonment, abuse, or neglect, children are usually placed in the custody of the state while efforts are made to reunite them with their birth parents or other relatives. If these efforts are unsuccessful, the public agency will petition the court to terminate the parental rights. In cases where birth parents are making a voluntary adoption plan, at least one of them, usually the mother, will execute a surrender of parental rights/consent for adoption. In some states, this may require a court appearance. In others, it only requires that documents be signed in the presence of one or more witnesses and a notary public. Each state has its own guidelines for when a voluntary surrender can take place and how much time must pass before it is irrevocable. These guidelines vary greatly. Some states, such as Colorado and Idaho, do not have any clear guidelines on when a consent can be signed or when and how it may be withdrawn. Other states require that surrenders only be signed after the birth of the child. Arizona statutes require that parents cannot surrender a child for adoption until at least seventy-two hours after his/her birth and then it is irrevocable. In California, a parent can surrender a child at any time after birth and revoke the surrender for a period of ninety days. (This information was obtained from the National Adoption Information Clearinghouse.) In all states, consents which have been obtained by fraud, duress, or other undue influence are subject to being overturned in court.

If the child's other parent, usually the father, does not voluntarily consent to the adoption, the agency or attorney must petition for termination of his rights in the appropriate court. If the mother does not know the identity of the child's father or chooses to withhold that information, she may be required to testify in court about her reasons. If the father of the child is known, a sincere attempt must be made to inform him of his rights. This might involve sending certified letters to his last known home or work addresses and/or advertising in the newspaper. Once he has been notified, he will have a specified period of time in which to claim the child. If he denies paternity or does not respond to notices sent to him, it will also be necessary to prove that he has not demonstrated an interest in the child. Interest is generally measured by factors such as:

- Living with the mother or providing for her support during the pregnancy.

- Living with the child or providing for his/her support.
- Acknowledging paternity by signing the birth certificate or filing a petition for legitimation.
- Registering on the putative father registry, if applicable.

Putative Fathers and Legal Fathers

If a child is conceived out of wedlock and the parents don't subsequently get married, the father may acknowledge paternity by signing the birth certificate or filing a petition for legitimation. If he fails to take either of these actions, he is referred to as the putative father. Even though he is not married to the mother, he has equal rights to the child in almost all states. If the mother was married at the time that she conceived the child or gave birth, her husband is the legal father. In cases where the legal father is not also the child's biological father, the rights of both the legal father and the putative father must be terminated. As recent highly publicized adoption cases have shown, failure to properly terminate the rights of the father can have serious consequences for the adoptive family and the child, so it is important to research such details thoroughly.

Putative Father Registries

In response to the need to protect the rights of unmarried fathers and the need to provide permanency for children placed in adoptive homes, many states have established Putative Father Registries. The implementation of the registries varies from one state to another but the basic function is the same. The registry serves as a means through which a birth father can have his intent to parent a child legally recognized. In most cases, he can register prior to the birth of the child.

Some states limit the amount of time for registration after the child's birth, in many cases it is thirty days. If an adoption placement is being considered for a child, the attorney or agency must check with the putative father registry to see if the child's father is listed. If he is, then he will be given the opportunity to claim the child or to be involved in the adoption plan.

Adoption Options

There have traditionally been two types of domestic adoptions that occur in this country: independent adoptions and agency adoptions. Both of these will be discussed at length in later chapters. There are many variations of each and all domestic adoptions will involve an agency and an attorney at some point. Some families will also seek the involvement of an adoption consultant or facilitator.

Independent adoptions   These adoptions are usually arranged by the birth parents and the adoptive parents, sometimes using an intermediary such as a family friend or an adoption facilitator. The involvement of an attorney is usually required to make sure that the legal rights of each member of the triad are protected. Independent adoptions are legal in almost all states. Depending upon the states involved, there may be one attorney for the adoptive parents and another attorney for the birth parents and/or the child. An investigation into the suitability of the adoptive home will be conducted by either a public or private agency or a licensed professional appointed by the court where the petition for adoption is filed. This investigation may occur prior to placement or after, depending upon the law of the state. In some cases, adoptive parents and/or the birth parents will receive counseling from an agency or another adoption professional before or after the placement.

Identified adoptions This is a variation on the independent adoption in which the adoptive parents and the birth parents have contact with one another and then go to an agency for services. The agency may provide counseling, medical care, transportation, housing assistance, and other services, usually at the expense of the adoptive parents. Many states prohibit adoptive parents or their intermediaries (other than licensed child-placing agencies) from paying for anything other than basic medical care for the mother and the baby. If an expectant birth mother needs help with her rent or food expenses during the pregnancy, an agency may need to supervise the payments. In an identified adoption, the agency enters into an agreement with the adoptive family and the birth parents that the child will be placed in that home, regardless of how many other families may be on the agency's waiting list.

Agency adoptions Adoption agencies may be public or private. They are licensed by the state in which they are providing services. Adoptions through agencies always require that the adoptive home study be completed prior to placement of a child.

Closed adoptions These are placements in which there is limited exchange of information between the birth and adoptive parents. Most, if not all, placements involving children who have entered the adoption system through abuse or neglect will be closed adoptions. Some private agencies still arrange closed adoptions, although with less frequency than in the past. In a closed adoption, nonidentifying information may be shared but birth and adoptive parents do not have contact with one another.

Open adoptions Most private agency and independent adoptions today involve contact between the birth and adoptive parents. In some cases, this may mean the exchange of letters and pictures and in other cases it may mean face-to-face meetings. Semiopen adoptions are those in which birth and adoptive parents meet at a neutral location, the agency or attorney's office, for example, and do not disclose their last names. In a completely open adoption, names and addresses are exchanged.

ADOPTIONS ACROSS STATE LINES

The placement of children from one state to another for foster care, residential care, or adoption is governed by the Interstate Compact on the Placement of Children (ICPC). The ICPC was developed in the late 1950s and New York was the first state to sign in 1960. Since 1991 when New Jersey signed, all fifty states, and the District of Columbia and the Virgin Islands, are members of the ICPC. The ICPC is a uniform statutory law that has been adopted by each state. The state where the child lives is known as the "sending" state and the state where the adoptive family lives is known as the "receiving" state. Each state has a specific person designated as the ICPC Compact Administrator. If you are considering adopting a child who has been or will be born in another state, you need to make sure that your adoption professional is knowledgeable about the guidelines of the ICPC.

The purposes of the ICPC are twofold: to provide protection for children and to provide protection for the states. It seeks to protect children through ensuring that the adoptive family is suited to care for a child, that the services needed to provide for the child's physical and emotional needs are available to the family, that the rights of the child's birth parents have been addressed, and that appropriate supervision will be provided after the placement. It prevents individuals or organizations from circumventing the laws of either state which protect the rights of the child and his/her birth parents. It seeks to protect states by ensuring that the sending state retains responsibility for the child until finalization of the adoption in the receiving state.

In order to arrange for an interstate adoption placement, the attorney or agency that represents the child must file an ICPC 100A form with the ICPC Administrator in the state where the child lives. Supporting documentation will probably include (some states may have additional requirements):

- proof of child's birth
- proof that the child is free for adoption
- proof of guardianship of the child (court order terminating parental rights, voluntary consent to adoption signed by one or both birth parents, interlocutory decree granting custody to an agency, etc.)
- medical and social history on the child and the birth parents
- adoptive home study for the prospective adoptive family

The ICPC Administrator will review the case for compliance with any applicable state laws. If there are legal risk issues, such as when the rights of one or both birth parents have not been completely terminated, it may be required that the adoptive family sign an acknowledgment of the risks involved. The adoptive home study must reflect that the adoptive parents are capable of providing for any special needs that the child may have. After the ICPC Administrator in the sending state examines the placement request and determines that it is complete, he or she will sign the 100A form and forward the file to the receiving state. The ICPC Administrator in the receiving state will review the case for compliance with any applicable laws in that state.

There must be a licensed agency or individual in the receiving state that has agreed to provide postplacement services and forward reports to the sending state via the ICPC Administrator. When the ICPC Administrator in the receiving state approves the placement, the family can then bring the child into their home.

Adoptive families must be prepared to wait for the necessary reviews and approvals to be completed before the child can move from one state to another. In private adoptions where the birth and adoptive parents have had contact with one another prior to the birth of the child, the adoptive parents may choose to remain in the state where the child lives until ICPC approval is completed. It can be very stressful for families to put their lives and their jobs on hold to go to another state to wait until their child can come home with them. In these situations, it is absolutely vital to have a knowledgeable professional assisting you. Filing the correct paperwork the first time around will reduce heartache for everyone involved. In some cases, birth and adoptive parents may choose to place the child in foster care during the waiting time. Adoptive parents may be able to visit the child frequently, but they cannot take him/her out of the state without the necessary approvals from both states. (Special thanks to Frank Barthel of the American Public Welfare Association.)

INDIAN CHILD WELFARE ACT

The Indian Child Welfare Act is one of the few federal laws which govern adoptions. It specifically requires that children who are of Native American Indian heritage cannot be placed in non-Indian families without tribal consent. It is important to ask your adoption professional about this law and how it might affect you.

REUNION REGISTRIES

The trend toward openness in adoption has resulted in the establishment of reunion registries in most states. There are also numerous private reunion registries around the country. The basic elements of a reunion registry are as follows:

- Adoptees must be adults (usually defined as eighteen to twenty-one years old) to initiate a search.
- Only adoptees or their biological siblings can initiate a search.
- Biological siblings can only initiate a search for an adoptee who is also an adult.
- Birth parents or other relatives cannot initiate a search.
- Consent of the birth parents is required for identifying information to be released to the adoptee.

In all states, adoption records will be kept on file permanently either by the agency that handled the adoption or the appropriate state agency. When adoptees inquire about background information, they will probably be able to receive any nonidentifying information right away. If they want to have more information or establish contact with birth parents, the consent of the birth parent(s) must be obtained. Since some states have only established reunion registries in the last fifteen years or less, birth parents may not know about the registries. If there is not a signed consent for release of information on file, the adoptee may be asked to pay a nominal fee to cover the expenses involved in locating the birth parent(s). If the person is found, they will have the option of having contact with the adoptee or maintaining their confidentiality.

It is important for adoptive families to know about the presence or absence of a reunion registry in the state where their child is born and/or the state where the adoption is finalized. If the birth parents have signed a consent for release of information at the time of the placement, they will be able to share that fact with the child later if he/she wants to search. If they haven't signed a consent, at least the adoptive parents will know what steps the child might need to take to initiate a search in the future.

I received a call a number of years ago from a woman who was inquiring about finding her husband's birth parents. I was working in a private adoption agency at the time and she had just randomly selected the phone number out of the yellow pages as a place to get started. She and her husband were in Atlanta for a business convention. He had been abandoned at the airport as an infant. He was subsequently adopted and was living in another state. Since he had always been interested in knowing more about his history, the couple had visited a local university to research the newspaper articles around the time that he had been abandoned to seek any bits of information that might help. When they went to the counter to request the newspapers, the clerk commented that it was interesting that only a few weeks prior, an elderly couple had been in requesting the exact same papers. The woman and her husband were convinced that the other couple was his birth parents (he was about forty-five). Upon further investigation, they learned that there had been an alumni meeting at another university a few weeks earlier. They had, therefore, deduced that perhaps his birth parents had been college students at the time of his birth. They were amazed by the possibility that fate had brought both of them to exactly the same spot within a few weeks of each other to look for information. I suggested that they contact the alumni association for the university to see if they could put an ad in the newsletter.

Private reunion registries allow for the birth parents, siblings, or other relatives and the adoptee to make their desire for contact known. There are numerous registries on the Internet where adoptees, siblings, and birth parents post pertinent information in hopes of finding one another or someone else who has knowledge of the adoption. These registries are very popular and many people are successful in locating family members who have been separated by adoption. For adoptees who have been abandoned, they may offer the only alternative for finding birth parents.

If you are just starting the adoption process, reunion registries and search issues may not seem that important to you. As your child grows up and begins to ask questions about his adoption and his history, you will be very glad that you made the effort to learn about what is available. Adoptees do not usually search for birth parents out of a dissatisfaction with their adoptive family, but more often out of a need to answer questions about their own identity. Most adoptees are very secure in their relationship with their adoptive parents and are not seeking to replace them with their birth parents. Many search organizations and professionals involved in reunion registries will recommend and offer counseling services to you and your child to help them through the search process.

LEGAL RISK PLACEMENTS

In cases where the rights of one or both birth parents have not been fully terminated prior to placement of the child with an adoptive family, there are legal risks involved. Some examples include:

- The birth parents have signed the necessary consents to the adoption but the waiting period for revocation has not passed.

- The rights of one parent, usually the birth mother, have been terminated through voluntary consent but the putative father has not been identified or located.
- The rights of the birth mother have been terminated but the putative father refuses to consent to the adoption because he denies paternity.
- The child is a ward of the state and the rights of both of the birth parents have not been terminated (see the section on adoption by foster parents).

In infant adoptions, there are many legal risk placements occurring today in both independent and agency adoptions. This is due, for the most part, to the requests of birth parents who are making adoption plans for their children. Although I have known and worked with many wonderful foster families, the foster care system seems to have a generally negative reputation in this country. Many birth parents do not want their child to spend any period of time in a foster home. If agencies have policies requiring children to be in foster care until parental rights are terminated, birth parents will usually seek independent adoption placements. Some believe that having the child placed with the adoptive family immediately will make the birth parents feel more secure about their decision and make it less likely that they will change their minds during the revocation period. Others believe that having the child in a foster home gives the birth parents time to evaluate their decision without feeling the pressure of trying to avoid disappointing the adoptive parents. It is a delicate balance and what is best for one set of birth or adoptive parents will not be right for another.

Some adoptive families will not be comfortable about taking a child into their home when there is any element of risk involved. They may, however, feel pressured to do so because they might not otherwise have a child. It is a difficult decision to set your own parameters for the amount of risk you are willing to accept. Your adoption professional should be able to help you establish some guidelines. You should also talk to other adoptive families in your support group to find out how they handled this issue and what the results were.

The most secure adoption placement will be a case where all parties who have legal rights to the child have signed consents or otherwise voluntarily surrendered their rights. The degree of risk inherent in situations that are not as clear-cut will depend upon the laws of the states involved. If the state has a putative father registry and the birth father has not registered within the time specified by law (in some states it is any time prior to or up to thirty days after the child's birth), or the birth father has been informed of the pending adoption and has chosen not to exercise his rights, the placement will be relatively secure. If, however, the birth father has not been named or the state does not have laws which specifically address the time limits during which he can claim the child, there is greater risk involved. In all states, adoptions can be overturned on the basis of fraud or coercion. The best protection of everyone involved is to work with licensed professionals who are experienced with handling adoptions.

FOSTER CARE AS A ROAD TO ADOPTION

As more and more emphasis has been placed on the child's need for permanency and stability, adoption professionals have encouraged the adoption of children by their foster parents whenever possible. This sounds unfair to adoptive families who have waited for years with their local public agency to even have a home study completed. However, the interests of the children are better served by remaining in the home where they feel secure and loved. When an infant or young child comes into the care of a public agency, every effort is usually made to find a foster family that would be open to adopting him/her in the future. Efforts to reunite families, locate birth parents, and terminate parental rights can take months or years, depending upon the laws of the state and the individual case. Imagine a two year old who has spent eighteen months in foster care before he/she becomes available for adoption, for example. He or she has spent most of his/her life bonding to the people who have cared for him/her and taught him/her to walk, talk, and explore his/her world. It would be far less traumatic for him/her to be adopted by his/her foster parents than to be moved into an adoptive family.

For many families, serving as foster parents to children who later became available for adoption has been a very rewarding experience. It allows them to bring the child into their home at a young age and influence as much of his/her development as possible. Because most public agencies have no or very minimal fees for adoption, the expenses are far less than those associated with independent or agency adoption. In some cases, adoption subsidies may be available on an ongoing basis to help the family provide for the child's needs.

Before you consider foster parenting as a means to adopt a child, you should be accepting of the possibility of the child being returned to birth parents or other relatives. You will not have any influence over the decision to return the child, it will be up to the legal system. If you feel that the child faces an uncertain future with his/her birth family, it will be especially difficult. Even if you know that he/she will be loved and adequately cared for, it is impossible not to be sad that he/she is leaving your home.

It takes a very special person to be able to do foster care. I have had the privilege of working with many wonderful foster parents over the years who never lost sight of the child's need to be loved and treasured. One really incredible family that I remember had three children. Their youngest son had been adopted and had lived in a foster home for a short time during the revocation period. They felt that being foster parents was their way of repaying what someone else had done for their son. However, they were not only involved in the care of newborns during the ten-day revocation period, they also cared for many infants, toddlers, and children who were in the custody of the state. Their philosophy was, "If we can make one day in this child's life better, then it is worth it." Over the years, I watched them take numerous children into their home who were later returned to their birth parents. Some of the children came back into foster care over and over again, and this couple always took them in. They never expressed bitterness toward the birth parents who couldn't provide a stable home or anger at the system that kept putting the children in jeopardy by giving the parents another chance. They calmly and faithfully remained focused on their goal of giving the children a safe and loving environment. In many cases, they even worked with birth parents after the children were returned, offering advice, babysitting, and just being supportive. One boy who was a foster child in their family off and on for many years was later adopted by them as a teenager. There are few people in the world who can open their hearts to others in this manner. However, children who need foster care desperately need parents like these. If you feel that you might be able to provide foster care, seek out advice from others who are experienced foster parents and follow your own heart.

The Court Appointed Special Advocate (CASA) program provides a wonderful opportunity for people who are interested in the foster care system to have some firsthand experience with how the system works. CASA volunteers are carefully trained to act as advocates in court for children entering the foster care system due to abuse or neglect. If you don't have the time to volunteer, you might still be able to talk to other CASA volunteers about their experiences and get some ideas about the special challenges faced by foster parents.

Chapter 7

Domestic Adoptions through Agencies

hild-placing agencies are licensed by the states in which they provide services. In most states, licensing is a very extensive process which may require that the organization be not-for-profit, have a Board of Directors which is representative of the community to be served, provide for an annual audit, meet minimum standards for staff qualifications, and provide for on-going staff training and development opportunities, in addition to many other regulations. Some states have standards of practice for the provision of services to children, birth parents, foster parents, and adoptive parents. Other states do not address issues relating to the provision of services in detail. You can check with your state adoption specialist or child-care licensing office (see chapter 11) for a copy of the regulations that apply to child-placing agencies in your state. It will give you an idea of what you can expect from the agency and what their responsibilities are.

THE BASICS OF AGENCY ADOPTIONS

- Families who choose to adopt through an agency will complete an adoptive home study prior to placement of a child.
- Guidelines for acceptance (age, marital status, etc.) will be determined by agency policy as well as by requests from birth parents.

- The demographics of the children placed by the agency may be determined by the agency's focus and funding sources.
- Adoption agencies (public and private) may be involved in recruitment of adoptive families for waiting children.
- Custody of children will be held by the agency until an acceptable postplacement period has passed to ensure adequate adjustment into the adoptive family.

The Process

The major differences between public and private agencies will be in the circumstances under which children become available for placement and the process of selecting an adoptive family. In general, adoptions through agencies will often follow a rather similar and predictable sequence of events.

Inquiry Verbal or written information will be provided to prospective parents about the agency's requirements and policies. Many agencies offer informational meetings or seminars free of charge and others have a nominal fee. If you meet the minimum requirements, you will probably be given a registration or application form to complete.

Intake After you file the registration or application form, the agency will let you know when you can expect to begin the home study and what will be required. In some cases, you may be asked to delay starting your home study until closer to the time that you can expect a placement. You may be asked to complete a form or write a letter giving basic information about your family. Adoption agencies usually maintain only a limited number of approved prospective adoptive families at any given time. As birth parents come to the agency requesting services, they need to be able to offer them several, in some cases many, possible families from which to choose. In many states, a home study is only valid for one year or until a child is placed and therefore agencies may be reluctant to complete home studies on too many families at a time because of the need for updates.

Home study There is a detailed description of the home study process in chapter 2. Adoption agencies often require participation in group meetings or training programs as part of the home study evaluation. During this time, you will be asked to come to a decision about the age and sex of the child you want to adopt.

Waiting for a child After you have completed all of the required paperwork, classes, and interviews, you will be placed in a pool of approved families. If there are children waiting for adoption that are within the age range you have specified in your home study, you might begin reviewing child information right away. If not, the length of your wait is very difficult to predict.

Placement of a child After a child has been identified for possible placement in your home, the agency will share information with you about his/her social and medical background. If you are accepting of the child, you may be asked to visit with the child prior to placement.

Postplacement Before you can finalize the adoption, you will need to complete a period of postplacement supervision. The duration and frequency of the supervision will be determined by the laws of your state and the policies of the agency involved. A detailed description of the postplacement process is found in chapter 10.

Finalization The adoption will be finalized in accordance with the laws of your state. You may need to have an attorney assist you with the filing of the adoption petition and termination of parental rights, if that hasn't already been completed by the agency. A new birth certificate will be issued for the child which will give your names as the child's parents and your county of residence as the place of birth.

Advantages to Using an Agency

Resources   An agency may have more contacts in the community which will help them to make more birth parents aware of their services. They will also probably use marketing techniques such as brochures, billboards, or ads in the telephone book.

Support   An agency can offer counseling and encouragement to both the adoptive parents and the birth parents. Most agencies have opportunities for their clients (birth and adoptive parents) to be involved in support groups either pre- or postadoption. For adoptive parents, it can be very reassuring to have someone they can call from time to time to ease their anxiety, especially if they're not being charged by the hour. Birth and adoptive parents each need to have someone who can advocate for their needs and desires. Working with an agency allows both parties to, hopefully, establish a close relationship with a professional who has experience with the questions and crises that may arise.

In cases where either party is reconsidering their decision about the adoption, it is especially helpful to have an agency worker acting as an intermediary. It allows each person the opportunity to explore their feelings privately without fear of risking the placement.

Security for the child   In many states, when a birth parent enters into a service agreement with an adoption agency, the agency will be responsible for assisting her in making a permanent placement for the child, under any circumstances. Even if it is not required by law, an ethical adoption agency will not abruptly terminate services to a birth mother. If a child is born with an unexpected medical condition, the adoptive parents previously selected for the child may not be able to accept him/her. In those cases, the agency will attempt to locate another family within its caseload. As a last resort, they will seek to locate a family through networking with other agencies or will refer the birth parents to an agency that can place the child.

Security for the adoptive parents   If you are working with an adoption agency, you may not be informed each time that a birth parent looks at your profile or considers you for placement of their child. This will save you the emotional wear and tear of having to experience each possible placement as a rejection. Depending on the circumstances, you may not even know about the child until all parental rights have been terminated and he/she is legally free for adoption. Also, you will not have as much of the emotional burden of making sure that everyone's needs are met.

Cost   Public agencies usually have no fees or minimal fees for adoptive families. Subsidies or other types of assistance may be available. Private adoption agencies usually charge set fees for their services. In most cases, adoptive parents do not pay the bulk of the fees until a child is actually placed in their home. If you adopt though an agency, you probably will not risk losing a lot of money for medical care and housing expenses in the event that the birth parents decide to raise the child.

Record keeping   Agencies prepare formal reports about a child's background, including medical, social, and emotional information. If you arrange an independent adoption, such information may only be communicated to you verbally and you might need to write it down and verify it yourself. Agencies are required to maintain adoption records permanently, usually in a fireproof file cabinet. If an agency closes, the records will be filed with the state's Department of Social Services (or equivalent). Records kept by facilitators or attorneys may not be subject to protection under the law.

Disadvantages to Using an Agency

Less control   Adoptive parents who like to be in charge may be frustrated by agency requirements and the length of time it takes to complete each step. You will also be relying on the agency to represent you to birth parents through your letters and pictures as well as their description of you. In an independent adoption, you might be talking the initial calls from birth parents yourself and therefore be better able to impact their decision about whether they want to meet you. Birth parents may also feel that they have less control when working with an agency and prefer to communicate directly with adoptive parents. Agency policies may be more restrictive and discourage legal risk placements that allow families to have children in their homes at very young ages.

Less flexibility   Agency policies may be restrictive with regard to age, length of marriage, number of children already in the family, etc. If you are single, over forty-five, or have several children already, you may have difficulty finding an agency that will work with you toward the placement of a young child.

Cost   Some adoptive families find that private adoption agencies' fees are higher than the costs incurred in some independent adoptions.

If you review the advantages listed above, you will see that an agency must invest a great deal of resources in making its services available to those who need them and for providing an extensive array of services. It is very, very difficult to anticipate what you will actually spend in a private adoption arrangement, especially if you are involved in numerous attempts before you actually complete an adoption.

Private Agencies

Children who are in the custody of a private agency will most often be those who have been voluntarily surrendered by their birth parents. The overwhelming majority of these children will be infants or toddlers. It is rare in our society for birth parents to make a voluntary adoption plan for a child who is beyond infancy, although it does occur. Private adoption agencies do not have the power to remove children from neglectful or abusive homes. They may, however, be involved in finding and preparing adoptive families for children who are waiting in the public foster care system. The trend toward privatization of services by local governments in recent years has resulted in some states contracting with private agencies to provide foster care and adoption services to children who are in public custody. In many cases, these agencies can take an active role in advocating for the families and the children. Final placement authority still remains with the state or local government agency.

When birth parents contact a private agency for services, there may be minimal or no fees involved. A caseworker will do an intake interview to provide information about the agency's programs and services and to assess the needs of the birth parent and/or the child. If the child has not yet been born, the agency will provide ongoing counseling to the birth parents during the pregnancy. Opportunities should be provided for the birth parent to explore the alternatives for the child, including but not limited to, adoption. Relationships with extended family members who may be able to help with raising the child should always be considered. If assistance with medical care, housing, transportation, clothing, or other items are needed, a contract for services will be established. In some cases, the caseworker will act as a labor coach for the birth mother. Contacting an agency during the pregnancy gives the birth parents time to establish a trusting relationship with someone who can be their advocate through the adoption process.

Preparation of the Profile

If you are adopting through a private agency, you will probably need to prepare a profile to be shared with the birth parents. The agency will guide you through the process of writing a letter about your family and selecting a collection of photographs of your family and your home. The profile will include information about your age, length of marriage, if applicable, other children, education, occupation, religion, and lifestyle. All information will be nonidentifying. Your profile and photographs should be prepared with care and attention. It will be your first chance to make an impression on a birth parent and will have a great deal of influence on whether or not they consider you for placement of their child. Letters should be simple and straightforward and should reflect your personality. Try to be as specific as possible about your lifestyle and how you plan to include a child. Tell about your extended family and friends and others who will be important in your child's life. Share information about your hopes and dreams for your child. Photographs should be of good quality, and you should choose those where you look happy and relaxed. You might want to include pictures of extended family members and/or pets as well.

The Selection Process

If the agency practices closed adoptions, there will probably be a committee of people who will make a decision about whether to offer a particular child to you for placement. The committee may consist of your home study worker, the worker for the child, and another, neutral, staff member such as the casework supervisor. Even in agencies that practice closed adoptions, birth parents will usually have some involvement in the type of family that is eventually selected for their child. If you are working with an agency that allows birth parents to be involved in the selection of parents, then your profile will be shown to birth parents who have requested a family like yours.

When working with birth parents to select an adoptive family, the agency worker will try to help them identify the most important factors for a happy family life. After they have developed some realistic parameters, the agency will show them some profiles, maybe two or three at a time. The birth parents will be asked to seriously consider each family. If they do not feel hopeful about any of the families presented, the worker will use it as an opportunity to help them develop more specific guidelines about the kind of family they want and then show them more profiles. If there are no families in the approved group that appeal to the birth parents, the agency will go through the intake forms and see if there is a suitable family waiting for a home study. If there is one, they will contact the family to see if they want to prepare a profile to be shared with the birth parents. If the agency does not have any waiting families that meet the requirements specified by the birth parents, they may network with other agencies to find a suitable family.

In a closed adoption, you will most likely not be offered a child for placement until after the rights of the birth parents, or at least the birth mother, have been terminated. In a semiopen or open adoption, you will probably be informed about the child's impending arrival and may be asked to meet the birth mother and/or father, and perhaps other relatives. In many cases, adoptive parents are present when the child is born or visit the child in the hospital shortly afterward. Some hospitals allow the adoptive family to pay for a room so that they can stay with the child.

Public Agencies

Children who are being placed in adoptive families by public agencies may have been voluntarily surrendered by birth parents who were unable to care for them or have been removed from their birth families due to abuse or neglect. Most of them will have spent time in a foster home or group care home prior to becoming available for adoption. Although involvement of the birth parents in the adoption process may not be possible, in many cases there will be other siblings or foster parents with whom the child will need to maintain contact. The agency will probably have extensive information about the child's background and medical history. Even in cases of abandonment, adoptive families should be able to obtain a lot of information about the child's progress in foster care. Many children who are awaiting adoption through public agencies are considered to be special needs children. They may have physical or mental disabilities, be of minority heritage, be older than infancy, or be members of a sibling group.

Photolistings and Adoption Exchanges

In the past few decades, photolistings and adoption exchanges have become a very effective way for waiting children to be united with adoptive families. Photolistings will include a picture of the child or sibling group and a brief description. If the agency has any specific requirements for the type of family being sought, it may be stated. Examples might include: a family that lives in a certain state so that the child can remain in contact with siblings who have been placed in other families; a family who has no other children younger than the child to be adopted; or a family that is active in a religion that is important to the child. Agencies generally strive to place as few restrictions as possible on adoptive families, while still respecting the individual needs of the child. Faces of Adoption: America's Waiting Children, is a computerized photolisting service provided by the National Adoption Center. It can be found on the World Wide Web at http://www.adopt.org/adopt. Photolisting books such as *Children Awaiting Parents* can be found in most public libraries. Many states have their own photolistings which are available in libraries or adoption agencies. Adoption exchanges include both waiting children and adoptive families. The National Adoption Exchange is administered by the National Adoption Center and has 115 members (adoption agencies, parent groups, and adoption exchanges) nationwide. Families with approved home studies can be registered on the exchange, and social workers all over the country who are looking for homes for children in their care can view their information. Video conferencing is also used in some areas to link adoptive families with children awaiting adoption.

The advantages to photolisting or adoption exchanges are significant. In the past twenty-five years, the National Adoption Center has helped to find homes for almost 7,000 children (information from Fact Sheet for Families published by the National Adoption Center). Photolistings allow prospective adoptive families to become familiar with children who may be in need of adoption. Learning about individual children may help some families to broaden their parameters about the child or children they will accept. Adoption exchanges are a tremendous resource for agencies because they allow social workers access to families throughout the country.

There are a few cautions you should be aware of when looking for a child through a photolisting. You must keep in mind that not all children listed will be available for placement in your home. Every effort is made to keep listings up to date and remove children for whom a placement is being considered. However, there will always be some delay between a family being identified for a child and the updating of the photolisting. It is, of course, possible that the agency will have numerous inquiries about the same child and you may not be selected as the most appropriate placement for him/her. Adoptive families should also be aware that, due to confidentiality issues, not all of the information about the child will be shared in a photolisting. Certain facts will only be given to those families who are genuinely interested in him/her and who meet the agency's requirements. Therefore, you may find out after inquiry that there are circumstances in the child's background that you cannot accept.

The Selection and Placement Process

In adoptions through public agencies, the selection of an adoptive family for a particular child is often made by the worker for the child or a committee of two or three staff members. If the child's foster parents are eligible to adopt him/her, they will probably have priority over other families. The child's personality, developmental level, medical condition, and special needs, if any, will be the main concerns in selecting an adoptive family. Agencies exercise a great deal of caution in trying to select an adoptive family that will be accepting of the child in order to avoid disappointment and emotional trauma for everyone involved.

In most cases, especially those involving children who are older than infancy, there will be preplacement visits. It is common for adoptive families to visit the child regularly over a period of weeks or months, gradually increasing the frequency and the duration. They might meet the child first in the agency office or the foster home and later take him/her for short trips to the local park or the zoo. Eventually, he/she may spend a night or a weekend in their home. If everything goes smoothly, the child will be placed permanently with the adoptive family. Preplacement visits provide the child and the parents with an opportunity to get to know one another and to feel confident about the adoption. Good preparation on both sides is essential to preventing adoption disruptions.

Adoption 2002

In 1996, the Clinton Administration announced plans to double the number of children in the public welfare system who are adopted or permanently placed by the year 2002. The plan of action calls for:

- Technical assistance grants to state agencies, courts, and communities to help them develop outcome-based approaches to permanency placement.

- Financial incentives to states for increasing the number of foster children placed in permanent homes.
- Aggressive implementation of the Multiethnic Placement Act (MEPA) which prohibits adoption agencies from delaying or denying placement of a child based on race, color, or national origin.

(This information was taken from a press release published by the U.S. Department of Health and Human Services.)

The Adoption and Safe Families Act of 1997 (P.L. 105-89) was signed by President Clinton on November 19, 1997. It is the first legislation resulting from the Adoption 2002 plan. It requires that the health and safety of children be the primary concern in the provision of all child welfare services, clarifies the circumstances under which reasonable efforts for family reunification need or need not be made, sets time limits for permanency planning hearings (within thirty days if reasonable efforts at reunification are not required, within twelve months in all other cases), and outlines when states must initiate proceedings to terminate parental rights. The law also encourages states to participate in concurrent planning for a child. This practice allows workers to identify and approve prospective adoptive families while a termination of parental rights petition is pending. It also promotes the placement of children in preadoptive families while waiting for termination of parental rights.

Chapter 8

Independent Domestic Adoption

*I*f mountains of red tape intimidate you and you would prefer to know your child-to-be's birth mother, independent domestic adoption may be the type your family opts for. Such adoptions are often free of the long waits of international adoptions and the bureaucratic procedures associated with large agencies. Independent adoption also allows you to get involved in the process, often alleviating feelings of powerlessness that can accompany other types of adoption.

THE BASICS OF INDEPENDENT ADOPTION

- Adoptive parents and birth parents may work together directly to arrange for the placement of the child.
- Most independent adoptions will be at least semiopen and will involve personal contact between the birth and adoptive parents.
- Adoptive parents often locate birth parents through networking, referrals from attorneys, facilitators, doctors or other professionals, or advertising.
- A few states do not allow independent adoptions; check your state's statutes.

- The services of an attorney are usually required to facilitate termination of parental rights.
- Some states allow placement of children in adoptive families prior to completion of a home study.
- Children may be placed in the adoptive home at a very young age, in many cases upon discharge from the hospital.
- All states will require a home study done by a licensed agency or individual prior to finalization of the adoption.
- Even if it is not required in your particular situation, it is highly recommended that adoptive parents request and pay for counseling for birth parents by a professional who is experienced in adoptions.

Communication

One of the first steps in an independent adoption is making a definite plan for handling communications with birth parents. Some families will choose to install a separate telephone line in their home, perhaps with an 800 number, to receive calls from birth parents. Others will choose to have their adoption attorney, agency, or facilitator handle the calls. Many families offer both options to birth parents so that they can proceed with whichever option feels most comfortable.

If you decide to handle the calls yourself, you will definitely want to have some guidelines from your adoption professional or your support group. Don't be overly concerned with getting all the details or eliciting a commitment from a birth mother on the first call. You should be friendly and supportive without being desperate or pushy. Building a relationship takes time and is easier if there is some type of emotional connection or similarity in personalities or values. Plan ahead of time how much information about yourself you are willing to share over the telephone and possible locations for a meeting. As you wrap up the conversation, make an agreement about whether there will be additional contact and how and when it will occur. If you receive a call from someone who describes a situation that is not acceptable to you, decline further contact. If you want to think it over, be honest and ask the person to call you back in a few days.

Networking

A popular method of locating a baby to adopt is networking with family, friends, and acquaintances. Adoptive families prepare a letter (see preparation of the profile in the chapter on agency adoptions) to send to as many people as they can think of regarding their desire to adopt a child. The letter should include information about your lifestyle, your motivation for adoption, your occupation, religion, etc. A photograph that includes all family members should also be provided. Some families send these letters to their professional colleagues and associates, friends, pregnancy crisis centers, college student unions, doctors' offices, and others. If the person who receives the letter is considering adoption or knows someone who is, they will contact the adoptive family or their intermediary. Anther method of networking is to distribute business cards that briefly state your desire to adopt a child to anyone with whom you have contact (store clerks, waitresses, etc.).

Advertising in Newspapers

According to the National Adoption Information Clearinghouse, thirty-two states allowed advertising by adoptive families in 1995. If you live in a state that does not allow advertising, you may be able to place an ad in a national newspaper or one in a state that permits advertising. Ads are usually short and simple such as: "Childless couple seeks to adopt a baby. We can provide love, security, and a wonderful extended family. Call 555-1212."

Advertising on the Internet

There are several websites on the Internet where adoptive families can list photographs and information to be viewed by birth parents who are considering adoption. Information about various sites can be found in the chapter on resources. One of the websites is Adoption Online Connection at http://www.adoptiononline.com. It was started in November of 1995 and, according to cofounder Allison Chidekel, there have been at least twenty-six successful adoptions as of March 1998. The site offers search features which birth parents can use to find families that meet their criteria. The search categories are divided up into groups such as family type (with or without children, single parents, multiracial families), adoption wishes (infants, twins, multiracial children, older, or special needs), geographical area (country, area of the country, state), family activities (pets, hobbies, recreation), lifestyle, religion, heritage, or occupation. Adoption Online Connection also advertises to adoption agencies, counselors, pregnancy centers, hospitals, and other organizations where birth parents might turn for help.

There are also resources where adoption facilitators or professionals list information about possible independent adoptions. Adoption facilitators often establish a network of adoption agencies or attorneys through which they attempt to match waiting adoptive families with birth parents seeking to place their children.

Advantages

- Adoptive parents are not limited by age or marital requirements set by agencies.
- Adoptive parents are more in control of the efforts to locate a child for placement in their home.
- Birth mothers and fathers are more in control of the selection of their child's adoptive parents.

Disadvantages

- Adoptive parents may be required to handle difficult situations without the support of an adoption professional.
- Adoptive parents may spend a lot of money on legal services and medical care, housing, etc. for a birth mother whose child they do not eventually adopt, for whatever reason.

Chapter 9

After The Commitment Is Made

$\mathcal{T}$he road to actually beginning the adoption process is a long one. You have made the decision to adopt, researched your options, interviewed agencies, attorneys, or facilitators, started filling out forms and begun making the financial and emotional investments required. Each step of the process is a commitment of time, emotion, and money. It is very important to trust your instincts and have faith in the chosen path. There may be unexpected complications and delays at any point and there will be many opportunities to question your choices. Adoption can be an emotional roller-coaster and you may begin to doubt whether you were meant to be a parent at all. The ability to laugh at life's little twists of fate, to seek support from those around you, and to persevere are absolutely necessary.

CONTROL ISSUES

The Serenity Prayer
"God, Grant me the serenity to accept the things I cannot change,
the courage to change the things I can, and
the wisdom to know the difference."

Many people find that this prayer brings them comfort in all aspects of their lives, and especially in a process over which they have limited control, like becoming a parent. It is helpful to look at each phase of the process and assess where your control ends. There will be people involved in an adoption, regardless of whether it is domestic or international, and each one has their job to do.

Regaining Control

Gathering all the information you need   Thorough research of your options will be of great benefit to you in the end. Take as much time as you need to contact agencies, talk to other adoptive parents, visit the library to read books and articles, and simply to think about your feelings toward adoption and parenthood. There is no right or wrong way to approach the process; some people need to have several months or even years to prepare themselves emotionally and financially prior to starting an adoption. Becoming a parent is a leap of faith, regardless of how your child joins the family, but there are some important issues you should look at before you leap.

Filling out forms correctly and returning them promptly   There will be reams of paperwork involved. Take the time to go through each form carefully and ask questions, as necessary. Make sure you sign everything. It is helpful to start a system of organizing your paperwork very early in the process. Some adoptive parents have told me that they had already amassed a file drawer full of agency brochures and adoption literature before they even started the home study. It is important to make copies of everything as you complete it, since some documents will be needed by two or three different entities. Try to separate documents into folders depending upon where they came from or where they were sent.

Preparing a thorough dossier or profile You should consider the preparation of your dossier or you profile package to be the most important job interview of your life. Letters and other documents should be carefully worded and should represent you in the best possible light. It takes a little longer to read and edit them several times, but it is better than throwing something together quickly and ruining your chance to make a good first impression. If you are asked to provide photographs, choose pictures where everyone looks happy and serene. It is a good idea to wear your best clothes. Depending upon the circumstances, you might be asked to provide photographs that depict your lifestyle and personality or photographs that are more formal. Follow the directions given by your agency or adoption professional as closely as possible.

Being available for interviews and classes It is not always convenient to take time off from work for home study interviews or to spend evenings at adoption classes, but your ability to work with the schedule set by the agency or practitioner is vital. Don't be intimidated by an employer who appears unyielding—if you were pregnant, you would be taking off for doctor's appointments. Be assertive, yet polite and firm in your requests for time off. When you are a parent, there will be many occasions when you will need to take time off because of a sick child, a special program at school, or an exciting field trip. The home study process is only the beginning of a lifetime of putting your family's needs first.

Staying in communication with your agency or facilitator If your agency or adoption practitioner does not have a regular means of communicating with you such as a newsletter, develop your own schedule for contacting them. Many adoption professionals carry a large caseload and the nature of their work involves many crises and urgent situations. Routine telephone calls to people who are in the waiting stage will have low priority. Many people struggle with the issue of how often to contact their agency without being a pest. If you have chosen a caring and professional agency or adoption practitioner, they shouldn't mind having you check in from time to time. A friendly call once a month may be a good rule of thumb to follow.

Keeping in contact with your agency or adoption professional will help you to feel connected to the process, even if there is no progress being made on your case at the time. It can be very reassuring to hear that adoptions are continuing to occur in the foreign country from which you are seeking to adopt, even though you don't expect to know about your child for several more months. You should also be able to confirm with your agency any information you get from other sources. When you are seeking to adopt a child internationally, you will suddenly notice every news article that comes along about that country and may begin to worry about how the political or economic situation may affect adoptions. If you are adopting domestically, you will be particularly sensitive to media coverage of new adoption legislation or placements that have been challenged by birth parents or other relatives.

You should also keep your adoption professional informed about trips out of town, job changes, moves, etc. If they need to reach you quickly, it is very important that they have the necessary information. Also, if your home study needs to be revised or updated prior to a child being placed in your home, it can be scheduled in a leisurely manner rather than completed in a rush when a child is actually waiting.

If you are participating in a mailing list on the Internet, you may hear about new regulations or procedures before or at the same time that your agency learns about them. If you are discouraged from calling the agency or if you sincerely feel that your adoption professional will not follow through on your case without constant prodding from you, then you have probably chosen the wrong professional or agency.

Building a support network There is great value in seeking out others who are also in the process of or have completed an adoption. They will be much more likely to understand what you are going through and to be able to offer support without needing to "rescue" you. Well-meaning relatives or friends who have no idea how the various bureaucracies work may feel the need to criticize the people or procedures involved for causing you so much pain and anguish. This is a natural response and is not usually intended to compound your feelings of frustration, but these attitudes generally do not serve to help you cope.

The Internet has revolutionized the entire adoption field, including the support group. Even if you live in a remote area where there are few adoptive families, you can communicate with thousands of people around the world if you have access to a computer. All social groups have their drawbacks and pitfalls, but many people report that they receive friendship, support, advice, and encouragement from their comrades on-line.

Educating yourself If you haven't already started, now is the time to begin learning about adoption, child development, discipline techniques, and perhaps the history and customs of the country in which you plan to adopt. Your time and energies in this area will not be wasted. If you are uncertain where to start, go to the library and check out any books that appeal to you or contact your local adoptive parent support groups, agencies, or child welfare organizations for information about activities and seminars in your community. If you don't have any resources available locally, contact some of the national adoption organizations for information on their annual conferences and plan to attend one. The North American Council on Adoptable Children (NACAC) holds its conference in a different location each year, to make it more accessible to everyone. The National Adoption Information Clearinghouse (NAIC) and Adoptive Families of America (AFA) can also provide information about conferences. If you are adopting internationally, start collecting packing lists and tips about the area where you may be traveling.

Taking time to care for yourself The adoption process is emotionally draining, as parenthood will be, so it is important that you make an effort to relax and recharge your batteries from time to time. If you are married, keeping up a good line of communication with your spouse is vital. Indulge yourself in your favorite activities now while you have the chance. See all those movies you have been meaning to see, read the newspaper, sleep late on Saturday, and finish those home renovation projects because all of these things will soon become distant memories once your child arrives. If you have medical concerns which need to be addressed or elective surgeries you have been postponing, take care of them before your child arrives.

Seeking to maintain a positive attitude Remember that no one is perfect and you should not be too hard on yourself when you experience occasional lapses of anger, despair, or grief. Hopefully, you will have a support network established to which you can turn for encouragement. You should make every effort to remain optimistic and focus your thoughts and attention on the life that you will one day share with your child. All of the delays and frustrations you experience along the way will be worth it in the end. Your attitude will have a big influence on everyone around you as well as your child. Keep in mind that this is part of his/her adoption experience also, and your ability to relate it to him/her in a positive way will be very important.

The following are areas where you will have little or no control.

Timetables Whether you are waiting for your certified birth certificates to arrive, for your social worker to finish typing your home study, or for a birth mother to decide whether she wants to meet you in person, you will be at the mercy of someone else's timetable. You will need to develop good coping skills and a lot of patience. Both of these will serve you well when you actually become a parent.

In a results-oriented society like ours, it is very easy to get caught up in wanting or expecting things to be done yesterday. In this situation, you have to do your best to complete any tasks for which you are responsible and then leave everything in the hands of others. There may be times when a gentle or not so gentle push is required, but choose your timing carefully and if possible, seek advice from others who are familiar with the process. Don't lose sight of your faith that everything happens for a reason.

Events As much as you would like to be able to plan how and when your child will arrive in your family, it will be totally impossible. If you are involved in a domestic adoption, the desires of the birth parents, the policies of the agency or the hospital, or medical complications for the mother or the child may dictate when and under what circumstances you first meet your child. If you are adopting internationally, you might be abruptly handed a tired and hungry infant shortly after you have completed a twenty-four hour journey. Even under less than optimal conditions, you can and probably will have a good experience. We all tend to think that the unexpected won't happen to us, but it is wise to at least consider how you would handle different situations before they arise. A good agency or adoption practitioner can help you know what to expect. If they can't give you the help you need, turn to your support group.

Recent books on pregnancy and childbirth encourage parents to make a birth plan that includes the type of anesthesia they want to use, how they plan to feed the baby, etc. Constructing an adoption plan is a great way to anticipate and discuss possible scenarios and alternatives. Keep in mind that all plans are subject to change at a moment's notice but at least you won't be caught completely off guard when the unexpected happens.

Information   You will probably want to have all the information you can get about your child's health history, family history, emotional and social development, fears, pleasures, and needs. There will, however, be many times when the information is not forthcoming. The reasons are many and varied. If your child has been abandoned, it may be impossible to get any information unless there was a note written by the birth mother. If your child lives in an area where he/she does not have access to advanced medical facilities, you may not be able to request all the tests that you need to make your decision about accepting him/her. If the birth parents of the child are afraid that you might not adopt him/her if you knew something negative about their pasts or the child's heritage, and they don't receive any counseling, they may not disclose all the information that you would like to have. It is essential that you can trust the professionals who are handling the adoption not only to give you all the available information but also to educate the parties involved about the importance of sharing information, both good and bad.

It is helpful to make a list of the questions you would like to ask your child's birth mother, foster mother, or other caretaker. Keep a notebook handy so that you can jot down things as they come to you.

That way, when the long-awaited moment finally arrives, you won't be completely at a loss for what to ask. You may only have one opportunity to get the answers to your questions, and adequate preparation may be vital.

Setting Goals and Evaluating Progress

Everyone likes to have some degree of structure in their lives and the ability to plan ahead. The very nature of the adoption process makes it very difficult to predict what lies ahead. You will have to put your job, your family life, and other things on hold while you are waiting for your adoption to occur. It can be a very stressful time. The following are some guidelines that will make the uncertainty a little easier to bear.

Set realistic goals If the agency or adoption practitioner you have chosen tells you that a home study takes two to three months, give yourself four to six. When there are delays such as smudged fingerprints that can't be processed or a reference who doesn't get his letter written due to a family emergency, you won't be devastated. Of course, if your report is written and approved within two months, you will be delighted.

Beware of anyone that promises timelines that are too concrete or that are very different from what you hear from others. Some agencies or facilitators have been accused, some rightly so, of using the promise of short waiting times to entice prospective adoptive parents into their programs. Take the time to check with the references provided and don't hesitate to seek out references on your own. There are many variables involved and it is impossible for anyone to provide you with a definite answer on how long it will take for you to adopt a child. It is, however, quite reasonable to expect an adoption agency or facilitator to tell you about recent cases and how long they have taken. Some agencies will offer to refund part of their fees if you do not have a child within a certain period of time. While this may be a good policy to have if you eventually withdraw from the program, it should not be the strongest motivation for choosing that program. You will probably remain with the agency much longer than the stated time, even if you don't have a child placed in your home, because of the emotional investment you have made. Your level of trust in the agency or facilitator and their services is a more important consideration.

Assess your progress regularly   I am one of those people who likes to be able to see physical evidence of concepts. I remember things by conjuring up images of them. When I worked in adoption agencies, I used a file-keeping system that involved placing files for families who were in the home study process in one section of the drawer, families with children assigned in another section, families whose children had been placed in another section, and so on. It was easy to look in the drawer and see how many children and families were still waiting to be united with one another. It was also very satisfying to move a family's file into the "child placed" section. If you like to visualize your progress, you might find it helpful to make lists of the tasks to be accomplished or milestones to be reached and check them off as they occur. If you don't like to make lists, it is helpful to use another tangible means of evaluating your progress. You might do this by talking it over with your spouse or a member of your support group. Try to identify specific milestones that have passed. It is easy to get overwhelmed by all the things that still have to happen before your adoption is completed. If you find that nothing has happened since your last assessment, review your original timeline. Are you still within the normal limits? If not, identify factors or circumstances that have caused a delay. If you cannot identify any reasons for the delay, don't panic—just give yourself a new deadline for reevaluation. If nothing has changed the next time you assess the situation, you might want to voice your concerns to your agency or facilitator.

Celebrate milestones It can be a wonderful stress-reliever to celebrate milestones in the adoption process. It may mean something simple like sharing the news with a close friend or something fancy like treating yourself to a new outfit or a day at the spa. Firsthand experience with the benefits of positive reinforcement will be an asset to you as a parent. You will find that celebrations, however simple, will give you the strength you need to face another day and answer the question, "Have you heard anything, yet?" at least one more time.

WHAT CAN GO WRONG?

There is often a very fine line between obsessing over all the possible negative outcomes of a chosen endeavor and taking the risk to try something. If you are frozen by the fear of the unknown, chances are you will never enter the adoption process at all. If you collect all the information you can, both positive and negative, and are still ready to try to adopt a child, you will probably be successful.

The old adage "Hope for the best and prepare for the worst" is good advice for prospective adoptive parents. The following list is not meant to discourage you from adopting a child, but rather to present you with possible challenges so you can begin to formulate your plans of dealing with them. Take a look at each one that might apply to you and consider what you would do if it happened. If possible, discuss some of these scenarios with your social worker or other adoption professional to see how similar situations have been handled in the past. Having a backup plan can make you feel stronger and more secure. It will also demonstrate to the person doing your home study that you have carefully considered the process and the responsibilities involved in becoming a parent through adoption.

- You lose your job
- You/your spouse get/s pregnant
- Paperwork gets lost in the mail
- Documents get misplaced in government offices
- A moratorium on international adoptions is announced in the country where you plan to adopt
- Birth parents or other relatives decide to parent the child
- The child is born with or develops an unexpected medical condition
- The child dies
- The adoption requirements in your state or the foreign country change, making you ineligible to adopt there
- Court dates are delayed
- Approval of the placement by the necessary governmental authorities is delayed
- Travel permission is delayed
- You can't accept the child after meeting him/her

Again, do not focus on the negatives, just be aware that all of the above can and do happen. You will meet many people in your adoption journey who have had smooth and uneventful experiences and you will meet others who have had horrible experiences. You can learn from both groups; take the advice that feels right to you and forget about the rest. Your experience will probably be somewhere safely in the middle.

What If Something Goes Wrong?

When the unexpected does happen, try to remain calm and carefully evaluate the situation and your options. Rely on your support network for advice and encouragement. You may need to consider the following issues.

Is my agency/facilitator/attorney providing me with all the information available? There can be some confusion about how much information is actually available or should be available. Confidentiality laws may protect the privacy of the other parties involved. Accurate medical information, for example, may be unobtainable. Refer to your original service agreements or contracts to see if everyone has lived up to their responsibilities.

Does my adoption professional seem to be knowledgeable and concerned? A simple measure is whether or not they return telephone calls in a timely manner. When you do have contact with them it is helpful to note whether they listen to your concerns and how they respond. Do they comply with your requests to meet in person to discuss your concerns?

Is there anything I can do to make things work out? You are your own best advocate. Follow your instincts and the advice of experienced adoptive parents or professionals in your efforts to effect change.

It is wise to use caution when contacting politicians for assistance. If you are waiting for your adoption hearing to be scheduled, for example, make sure that the judge or court clerk has all the necessary documentation before having your legislator call on your behalf.

If you feel that you or your child are not getting the services that you need, you will need to formulate a plan of action. It is always a good idea to get objective advice from others before you take any action. You will probably have a great deal of money and emotion invested in the adoption process and you should try to work things out with your chosen adoption professional whenever possible. If there is a grievance procedure, follow it. If you can take your concerns to the agency's Board of Directors or the state licensing officials, you might consider doing so.

The following story was shared with me by an adoptive family that prefers to remain anonymous:

> "As we begin the process of adopting our second child, we remember the ups and downs of our first experience with adoption from China. Initially, everything went very smoothly. We gathered all the necessary documents and sent our dossier to China and got ready to wait. To our surprise, just six weeks later on the Friday before Mother's Day, we received our referral. Our daughter was close to seven months old at that time. She was healthy, beautiful, and best of all, almost ours! Our agency told us to expect to travel in about three months. I was busy completing my dissertation and wondered how we would get a nursery ready and make all the necessary travel arrangements in time to go. Little did I know then that I would have much more time to get ready than I would ever need!

"The first two and a half months of waiting passed by quickly. With great excitement and anticipation, we managed to get everything done from dissertations to painting a crib to buying fun gifts for those who would help us in China. I called our social worker occasionally to check in and to find out which travel groups had been given approval. Although it never seemed fast enough, groups were receiving permission to travel and were arriving home with their new children. When three months had come and gone, I started checking in with others who had received their referrals at the same time as we did. To my dismay, most of them had received travel approval and were making final preparations for departure. All of the prospective parents, our social worker, and agency representatives were quite reassuring at this point, telling us that the adoption ministry in China often gives approval for travel 'out of order'. We were told to hold tight and that we would no doubt hear something soon. This was something we ended up hearing many, many times over the next six months until it was discovered that our dossier had somehow gotten lost when the adoption ministry in China moved.

"It is still painful for me to think about that six months. As many times as we had been told to prepare for the unexpected with international adoption, I don't think I could have ever prepared for the worry, anger, and grief that I experienced during that time. I worried about our daughter-to-be. We knew that she was in foster-care, but long periods of time would elapse in

between reports about her health. At times I wondered
if she was still alive or if she had been adopted by
another family. At one time, we were told that she had
been moved to a rural village where the level of her care
was questionable. I worried about her ability to attach
to new parents the longer she remained with her foster
family. Sometimes I had doubts about my own ability
to bond with a toddler rather than an infant. I was angry
at our agency, our social worker, and sometimes at
myself for letting myself care so much about a daughter
who was hardly real yet. All I knew of her was from a
handful of photographs, but with each passing day, she
felt more like my daughter. Yet if I had a daughter, why
couldn't I hold her, feed her, and comfort her? With
each milestone or marker that passed, I grieved for the
loss of our time to be in relationship with our daughter.
During the nine months that we waited to travel, our
daughter learned how to walk, celebrated her first
birthday, outgrew two sizes of clothes, missed her first
Christmas with us, and learned how to say her first
words. Much of the time my husband and I felt very
alone with our grief and we struggled to remain hopeful.

"As time went on, I became increasingly more
convinced that something had gone wrong with the
process in China and begged for someone to intercede
on our behalf, but our agency seemed to make little
to no effort to investigate the situation. Our social
worker listened sympathetically, but could offer no help.
When we finally received word that the problem had
been discovered and was being worked out so we could

travel, it was difficult for me to feel excited for fear of another disappointment.

"Fortunately, there were no other setbacks and we traveled to China more than nine months after receiving our referral. From the moment that our daughter was placed in my arms, the anguish of the previous months began to heal.

"We have been a family now for over a year. During that time, our daughter has blossomed from a malnourished, grieving sixteen-month-old into a healthy, active, and talkative two-and-half-year-old! We've recently decided that we feel ready to start the process again, in part, so that our daughter will have a sibling. Mostly though, we've found our lives to be so enriched by the addition of our daughter that we want another child to complete our family. After much thought and conversation, we have decided to use the same agency for our second adoption. In spite of our personal unhappiness about the way that our lost dossier was handled, we hold our agency in high regard for a number of reasons. Foremost, we respect the ethical way that our agency works with child welfare systems in other countries. We also think that the staff members who work in China are wonderful people who we would like to see again. Finally, we feel somewhat more prepared to handle the unexpected this time around. We know that one way or another, we will be united with the child who will become a member of our family. With any luck, a lost dossier won't be part of the process this time!"

Chapter 10

Homecoming and Beyond

$\mathcal{E}$veryone seeking to become parents, whether for the first or the tenth time, must ask themselves if they are ready to share their lives with a child. While it is impossible to know beforehand what challenges and rewards lie ahead, it is crucial to have a desire to nurture and guide a child's development, patience, flexibility, and tolerance of differences. Prospective adoptive parents may also wonder whether they have the capacity to love a child who was not born to them. For the majority of adoptive parents, their fears are quickly forgotten once the child is placed in their arms and they begin to realize the enormity of their responsibility to the child. Because of the dependent nature of the relationship, most parents instinctively feel a need to protect and nurture their child. The facts of biology or adoption have little impact on the strength of the emotional bonds between parents and their children.

ENTITLEMENT

One issue with which adoptive parents must come to terms is that of entitlement. They may have nagging doubts about whether they were meant to be parents. Occasionally, these doubts are reinforced by people close to them. One parent shared with me that the women in her church had discouraged her from adopting because God did not want her to have a baby. It is important to acknowledge these doubts and discuss them with a spouse, adoption professional, or close friend throughout the adoption process. Each delay or obstacle can cause these issues to resurface and you may need to resolve them again. Even after a child is placed, the adoptive parents may hear comments like, "Couldn't you have children of your own?" Most people do not even understand how hurtful a comment like that can be.

Feelings of entitlement are furthered by claiming behaviors. These behaviors help the parents and the child to feel that they belong together. A common means of claiming a child is by acknowledging how he/she is similar to the parent. Such similarities are further reinforced by comments such as "He looks just like you!" While such statements seem simple and trivial, they go a long way in making the parent feel connected to the child. In adoptive families, even though family members may not share similar physical characteristics, it is often easy to identify qualities that the members have in common, e.g., "She is feisty just like her dad."

Joining support groups for waiting parents and sharing your fears, anxieties, and hopes with others who are in the same situation can be very beneficial. If there is no support group in your area, you may find that you can get the support you need from joining one of the many adoption mailing lists on the Internet. Thousands of people have made close friendships through their involvement with such lists. As you become acquainted with others who share a common goal of building their family by adoption, you will find that your feelings are not so unique. It is very comforting to be able to share your anxieties with others who are not in a position to judge you.

Prospective adoptive parents have often experienced many disappointments prior to entering the process. It is only natural to be reluctant to believe that the adoption will actually happen. Even adoptive parents who have not been through the pain and loss of infertility know that the road to becoming a parent is never easy or predictable. Many people find it comforting to celebrate each step of the process by buying something for the child. If the age and sex of the child are unknown, there are still many items that can be purchased in advance such as books, tapes, and decorative items. The act of collecting things for the child helps the parent feel a connection to their child and deepens the belief that it will happen.

BONDING

Bonding is the instinctive need to protect another person that everyone, hopefully, will experience toward those who are close to them. It is a process rather than an event. The bond is the foundation upon which the relationship and attachment are built. It helps you remain committed to your child even when he/she does not react to you in the way that you had hoped. Women seem to be more likely than men to begin bonding prior to the birth or adoption of a child just because of the emotional differences between the sexes. Adoptive parents who have spent many years planning and hoping for a child often feel pressure to experience love at first sight. It is perfectly normal, however, for anyone not to experience overwhelming love for a child upon seeing him/her for the first time.

For couples expecting a child by birth, there are physical changes that make the child's imminent arrival easily known. Friends and even strangers give positive feedback and encouragement. Prospective parents shop for the new baby and begin to make plans for child care, revised work schedules, and so forth. For couples adopting a child, there is much less tangible evidence of impending parenthood and therefore less support from others. Many prospective adoptive parents are hesitant to tell people about their hopes for adopting, for good reason. It can be very emotionally draining to have well-intentioned coworkers continue to ask, "Have you heard anything yet?" Some people find that it is less stressful to tell only a few people about the adoption. Others tell everyone who will listen, in their excitement about having a child. They often find that many of their acquaintances have been touched by adoption in one way or another (have adopted, know someone who has adopted, etc.) and receive a lot of positive encouragement and support. Individual differences need to be taken into consideration before deciding when to tell others and how much information to share.

As a person moves through the adoption process, he/she may begin to fantasize about what their child will be like in the same way that a biological parent does. I have had many tearful calls from women who became pregnant while waiting to adopt a child. In almost all cases, they were grieving the loss of the adopted child to whom they had been bonding for several months. Once a child is identified and a picture is received, parents begin bonding to the photo and giving the child personality traits based upon his/her appearance. Of course, photographs may be of poor quality and the parents may be surprised that they don't like the way the child looks. Many times the child who appears shy and forlorn in a photo is actually very self-confident and active. When adoptive parents meet birth parents, they begin to formulate ideas about what the child will be like based upon the personalities and appearance of the birth parents.

ATTACHMENT

Attachment refers to the relationship that develops between two people where they begin to trust one another and prefer each other's company over that of others. As children learn that their parents will be there to meet their needs and are trustworthy, they become more and more attached. At different developmental stages, children go through periods of stranger anxiety where they may demand to be in the parent's presence at all times or refuse to interact with anyone else. Although it can be physically and emotionally tiring to have a one year old who won't let you put him/her down, it is a sign of healthy attachment that he/she realizes that he/she does not want you to leave him/her. Children who have experienced an attachment to a caretaker who responds to their needs are more likely to be able to form attachments with others. If the child you adopt has been in a foster home or institution, it is a positive sign for him/her to protest vehemently to the loss of those important people. It means that he/she has been loved and that he/she will have the capacity to love you just as deeply.

Children who suffer from attachment disorders, on the other hand, do not have strong connections to their caregivers. They are often described as children who will go to anyone without looking back. There are big differences between confident, outgoing children who know that their parents are close by and those who are indiscriminately friendly and don't look to their parents for support. Attachment problems may be overcome by spending lots of one-on-one time with the child. For older children who have missed the holding, cuddling, and rocking of infancy, these behaviors may be very beneficial. Giving the child the love and care that he/she missed at an earlier developmental stage is important in helping him/her catch up emotionally. Providing for the child's daily care strengthens the parent's confidence in his/her ability to care for the child and it strengthens the child's sense of trust that the world is a safe place.

PREPARING THE OLDER CHILD

When adopting an older child domestically, most, if not all, agencies require preplacement visits, sometimes for a period of several weeks or months. These visits may be at the foster home, the agency, or the adoptive family's home. Visiting a child in the foster home helps the parents to become familiar with his/her previous environment and allows them to have discussions with him/her about the foster family, his/her neighborhood, pets, friends, etc. It also allows the foster parents to show him/her that they approve of the adoptive parents and thereby give him/her "permission" to accept them. It is very helpful for children to have photos of the adoptive family and their home and community so that he/she can become familiar with them prior to placement.

In international adoptions, the preplacement visits may take place over a period of only a few days or not at all. The adoptive parents may simply arrive one day and take him/her to a hotel or other temporary residence while the adoption is being processed. Photo albums, which can sometimes be sent before the family travels, are a wonderful way for the child to begin to get acquainted with their new home. Photos should reflect the interests and lifestyle of the family and include pets, important places such as school or church, and perhaps grandparents or other extended family members. One mother I know made a copy of a referral photograph of her child and cut him out of the picture and pasted his image onto a picture of his room. The child was delighted when he arrived in his new home and saw his bedroom exactly as it was in the picture. If parents have toys, stuffed animals, or dolls for the child, they may take pictures of them and then take the toys with them when they travel so that the child has something familiar. This is a good project for other children who are already in the family to be involved in also. In some cases, the child's caretakers may decide not to share the photo album with him/her until you actually arrive. They may be afraid that the child will be devastated if something happens and the adoption doesn't work out. They may also be concerned about his/her inability to understand time and the emotional ups and downs he/she may experience waiting for something that he/she may believe won't happen, at times. Even if your child doesn't see the album until you arrive, he/she will still have the time that you are in his/her country waiting for the adoption to be processed to study the pictures and ask questions. It is always a good idea to make two or even three copies of the photo album, in case one gets lost or destroyed. Orphanage workers or foster parents might really appreciate having a copy also.

EASING THE TRANSITION

After you have survived the home study, the search for a child, the wait for a court date or travel approval, the anxiety of the revocation period, and whatever else might have come your way, you are finally ready to bring your child home. Hopefully, you have used your time wisely and have read books on parenting, discipline, and adoption, have done your research on the Internet, and have made contact with other parents. You can never be too prepared, although you may have reached many points at which you just couldn't look at another picture of a smiling baby or another crib ensemble. Even though you feel like you've aged a thousand years, your life with your child is just beginning.

Make the Transition Go as Smoothly as Possible

Find out as much as possible about your child's previous schedule and try to provide the same routine if you can Children of all ages thrive on structure. If your child has been in foster care or an orphanage, ask questions about his/her routine, how he/she likes to be comforted, how he/she falls asleep, what are his/her fears, etc. It is always a good idea to write these questions down prior to the actual placement, so you won't miss the opportunity to get information that may not be available later. If he/she has a comfort object such as a blanket, pacifier, or special toy, try to make sure that he/she is allowed to keep it. If he/she doesn't have a special comfort object, you might want to introduce one. A soft toy or a music box are good items to use.

Keep your expectations for yourself and the child realistic   Whether a child joins the family through birth or adoption, parents often report surprise and even guilt at their lack of instant love. This is perfectly normal and is not, by itself, a cause for concern. Parents should be kind to and supportive of one another and allow their relationship with their child to grow in an atmosphere of peace and harmony. Children should be allowed to express their fears and anxieties or even displeasure with the placement and be reassured that their parents will be there for them. Problem behaviors can be worked out over time.

Limit visitors   Although everyone is understandably eager to meet your new child/children, it is important that the little one attach first to mom and dad and feel secure that they will be there to meet his/her needs. This is most easily accomplished by having the parents provide for all of his/her care for the first few weeks or months. Treat the situation the same as you would if you had given birth to the child, regardless of his/her age. The postpartum period for most families is a time of devoting total energy and attention to making sure the new baby's needs are met. Parents will spend their time cuddling, rocking, holding, and singing to their baby. Newly adopted children, at any age, need to feel surrounded by love in order to develop a sense of security. If relatives or friends are anxious to help, ask them to prepare casseroles, do a load of laundry, or run errands.

New parents need time to work out their relationship with their children and build confidence in their own parenting skills. Some people find the help of relatives invaluable at this time and others find it intrusive. Evaluate your own personal style beforehand. If family gatherings usually have you feeling that you need to entertain everyone and make sure that everything is perfect, it's probably better not to have your relatives come for an extended visit when your child arrives. If you enjoy a relationship where all family members pitch in together and no one has to be in charge, then you may feel grateful for help from your relatives. Especially if you have traveled overseas to adopt your child, it is nice to have grandparents around who can assist with the chores of running the household while you and your child recover from jet lag.

Keep the household quiet Adjust the volume on telephones, televisions, radios, and anything else that might cause overstimulation or excitement. Noise and confusion can be very stressful for anyone but especially for a child who has found himself/herself in an unfamiliar environment. If your child has previously lived in an institution, he/she may experience a period of sensory overload and keeping the noise level to a minimum can help tremendously.

Allow for grieving You may have spent months or probably years in your journey to adopt a child. Of course, you hope that your child will bond to you immediately and know how much you love him/her. The reality is that all children need to be allowed to grieve for their previous home regardless of how long they were there or what the conditions were. This is especially true for children who are beyond a year old at the time of placement. For them, it is a real possibility that your loved ones can disappear at a moment's notice. It may take them months or even years to feel really secure and convinced that you won't suddenly be gone forever.

With older children, there is often a honeymoon phase in which the child is on his/her best behavior and everything seems wonderful. I have had many parents report to me within a few weeks of their child's placement that they are so well-behaved, clean up after themselves, etc. Later on, usually within a few months, the child becomes more comfortable in his/her new home and more certain that his/her adoptive parents will not send him/her away. He/she may then begin to display more annoying behaviors that make the parents feel that they have done something wrong to "ruin" their terrific kid. Actually, it may be a positive sign in that the child feels secure enough to make a few mistakes. In some cases, however, the child may have realized that he/she really likes his/her new home and becomes fearful that he/she will lose it. He/she may be, consciously or subconsciously, acting out deliberately as a defense mechanism. The idea is that he/she may be trying to get the parents to send him/her back sooner rather than later when he/she has become even more attached. Whatever the reason for the misbehavior, parents need to be firm and consistent in letting him/her know that they love him/her but do not love his/her behavior.

Sometimes adoptive parents become so immersed in the process of finding a child to adopt and all the necessary paperwork that they forget or don't allow themselves to prepare for the job of parenting. In the mid 1980s, my job involved handling adoptions in El Salvador. A civil war was underway, and adoptive families were not required to travel there to complete adoptions or pick up their children. As a result, many adoption agencies arranged for children to be escorted to the United States. Escorts were usually agency staff or airline employees who could travel free or at a discounted fare. A couple, who I'll call Bill and Cecilia, was working with me to adopt their first baby. Their son, Randy, was born on July 4, chubby and healthy. At the time, Legal Guardianship orders were being granted to allow children to come to the United States for adoption. However, shortly after Randy's birth, there were some changes in the laws pertaining to international adoption and his case was delayed for several months. Every week, Bill would call me for an update. Each time I would give him whatever new information I had and tell him what the attorney in El Salvador anticipated would happen next. Bill was always understanding and pleasant. He would always say, "Well, we'll just have to be patient." When the case was finally resolved and Randy was ready to come home to his new family, the attorney's wife brought him to Atlanta. An airline stewardess had volunteered to take him to Boston, where Bill and Cecilia would be waiting. Since they lived only about thirty minutes from the airport and the flight from Atlanta would take at least an hour and a half, I had told them to stay at home and I would call them when Randy and the escort had gotten on the flight. If they weren't able to get seats as standby passengers, they would try the next flight. Everything went like clockwork and I called Bill to let him know that his son was safely en route to Boston. His response was, "Okay, when he gets here, what should we do? My wife has been telling me all along that she knew all about babies but this morning she admitted that she doesn't know a thing!" Of course, I told him to stop on the way to the airport and buy formula and diapers and then call his mother! Randy has grown up into a handsome and intelligent young man, so his parents' lack of experience obviously didn't prevent them from doing a wonderful job.

POSTPLACEMENT AND FINALIZATION

Postplacement supervision refers to the contacts held between the adoption professional and the family after a child has been placed in the home. The purpose of postplacement supervision is two-fold: it should confirm to the individuals or organizations who arranged the adoption that the child is being adequately cared for and is adjusting into his/her new family and it should provide an opportunity for adoptive parents to obtain answers to questions that may arise. Visits always include at least one parent and the child and most states/agencies require at least one visit that includes all members of the household. The frequency of the visits and the duration of the postplacement period will depend upon the laws of your state, the laws of the child's home state or country, and the type of adoption you are completing.

Some adoptive parents may feel that postplacement supervision is yet a further invasion of their privacy. It is helpful to keep in mind that it is very rare that a child is removed from his/her adoptive home. After having been through all the necessary screening and preparations prior to placement, most adoptive families are quite capable and committed to their child. All parents, regardless of whether their children joined the family through birth, marriage, or adoption, struggle from time to time with the responsibilities involved and wonder about their abilities. Adoptive parents have the added burden of feeling that they have to be super parents and not admit to any frustrations or doubts. If you have chosen a social worker with whom you have established a good rapport, you should be able to use these contacts to explore your concerns as well as receive support and encouragement. Many agencies have postplacement groups where families can benefit from one another's experiences.

Independent Domestic Adoptions

In some states, children may be placed in adoptive homes by their birth families without an adoptive home study having been completed. The home study and the postplacement supervision in those situations is often provided simultaneously and may consist of only one home visit. The focus of the contacts is usually based upon making sure that the minimum requirements for an adoptive home have been met and little or no education is provided. If you are completing an independent adoption, your involvement with an adoptive parent support group or attendance at adoption seminars will be even more valuable because you will not have the benefit of learning from the experience that an agency may have to offer.

Domestic Adoptions Through Agencies

In agency adoptions, the consent of the agency (public or private) that has custody of the child must be given in writing prior to finalization. Such consent is given only after the successful completion of a postplacement supervisory period. The duration of the postplacement period will vary depending upon state laws, agency policies, and the presence or absence of problems. A good rule of thumb is two to four visits over a period of six months to a year.

It seems almost contradictory that adoptive families who have been subjected to close scrutiny by an agency prior to the placement should have more postplacement supervision than families who haven't even completed a home study. Our society has a long tradition of upholding the rights of the individual and this belief has and will continue to affect child welfare laws and policies. The basis for the discrepancy in the way in which adoptions are handled is the premise that birth parents are better qualified to decide what is right for their children. Adoption agencies don't disagree with that principle, they just usually operate on the philosophy that everyone, being human, is apt to make mistakes, and children are at less risk of abuse, mistreatment, or disruption of the placement if the adoptive family is carefully screened and prepared in advance.

International Adoption

The requirements for postplacement supervision and reporting may not be enforceable in international adoptions, especially if the adoptions are finalized overseas. In all cases, there will be a request from the foreign government for follow-up reports. In some cases, adoptive parents will sign an agreement to provide the reports as part of the finalization process. In other cases, agencies here are asked to provide a written promise to provide postplacement services before the family can even be considered for placement of a child. Please do not take these promises and agreements lightly! Postplacement reports and, especially, pictures of happy children who are thriving in their families are essential to the continuation of international adoptions. There will always be, from time to time, negative stories about adoption. Some of them will be true and others will not. If the individuals responsible for the adoptions don't have solid evidence to prove that the vast majority of placements are successful and beneficial, the adoption system may be in jeopardy.

If you adopt a child from a country where the adoption is not finalized overseas, the requirements for postplacement may be determined by the foreign child welfare officials and/or the U.S. agency. In some countries, such as the Republic of South Korea, guardianship of the child is given to the U.S. agency. The agency will consent to the finalization of the adoption just the same as if it had been a domestic adoption. If you don't live in a state where the child-placing agency is licensed, the requirements of the Interstate Compact on the Placement of Children (ICPC), which is discussed in detail in chapter 6, will apply. In other countries, legal guardianship is given to the adoptive family. This creates a cloudy legal situation in some states. If the person who has custody of the child must consent to the adoption, how can the adoptive parents consent to their own adoption? Some agencies resolve this problem by having the adoptive family surrender the child to the agency so that the agency can consent to the adoption. In other states, it is acceptable for the agency to submit a statement of agreement or concurrence with the adoption plan rather than an actual consent.

If you adopt a child in a country where the adoption is finalized overseas, you may need to complete postplacement supervision in order to finalize the adoption in your state. If both parents did not personally see the child prior to the adoption overseas, the adoption must be finalized in the United States before the child is eligible for citizenship. Some states require that the family complete an adoption finalization as if it were a domestic placement and others require only an affirmation or domestication of a foreign decree. The former normally requires a court report from a public or private agency which confirms that all of the state's requirements have been met and that the home is suitable for the child. The latter may only require proof that the child has been lawfully admitted to the United States and that the adoption has been completed by competent authorities overseas. If both parents traveled abroad and saw the child prior to the adoption, they are not required to adopt the child in their state. It is, however, strongly recommended that you do so because it will establish a legal record of your child's adoption that can be accessed at any time during his/her life when he/she may need a certified copy of his/her adoption decree. It may be very difficult, if not impossible, to get additional copies from the child's country of birth if your original copy is lost or damaged. Another reason to finalize the adoption locally is that many states provide birth certificates for children adopted internationally. Some states will issue the new birth certificate only after the adoption is finalized here and others will issue them upon submission of the appropriate forms and copies of the foreign decree. Having a birth certificate issued by the local Registrar of Vital Statistics does not automatically make the child a U.S. citizen, but it does make it much easier for him/her to obtain certified copies of his/her birth certificate as he/she needs them.

CITIZENSHIP

For detailed instructions on obtaining citizenship for your adopted child, see chapter 4. It is strongly recommended that you apply for citizenship as soon as possible after your child arrives in this country and certainly within the first two years. After your child has received his/her Certificate of Citizenship, you need to apply for a U.S. passport right away, even if you don't plan to travel out of the country. Having a file with the U.S. passport agency will be further evidence of his/her citizenship if anything ever happens to the INS file. You can never take too many precautions to document your child's legal status.

Chapter 11

Resources

*T*he most confusing and overwhelming part of the process may very well be where to start looking for the information you need. There is a great deal of information available, you just need to be prepared to talk to lots of people and read lots of material. I have not included specific information about agencies, attorneys, or facilitators in this chapter but you will find many references to places to receive up-to-date lists. Please keep in mind while you are doing your research that lists may be outdated from one day to the next. When you request information from someone or view websites on the Internet, check the date that it was last updated. You will still need to contact references, licensing officials, the Better Business Bureau, and any other appropriate sources to confirm that the information you obtain is accurate and reliable. In general, adoption professionals who belong to professional organizations are more well-informed and more experienced. Agencies or individuals who have been accredited will generally adhere to a higher standard of practice than those who are not. There are, however, many reputable adoption professionals who are not accredited or members of organizations.

ORGANIZATIONS:

Adoption Oklahoma
http://www.boonesmith.com/adoptok/
E-mail: rdinkins@ix.netcom.comAdoption Travel.com
http://www.adoptiontravel.com
E-mail: feedback@adoptiontravel.com

The Adoptive Parents Committee (APC)
http://www.wp.com/apc.home.htm
E-mail: alapc@aol.com
Adoptive parents support group in New York, with members from Connecticut, New Jersey, and Pennsylvania as well.

Adoptive Families of America (AFA)
2309 Como Avenue
St. Paul, MN 55108
1-800-372-3300
(612) 645-9955
Fax: (612) 645-0055
http://www.adoptivefam.org
This is a nonprofit group that provides a wealth of resources, including listings of agencies, information about laws relating to adoption, listings of adoptive parent support groups, etc. either free or at a very low cost to anyone interested in adoption. They publish Adoptive Families Magazine, a bimonthly magazine which contains articles from adoptive families, birth families, foster families, and professionals. They also conduct periodic national adoption conferences.

American Academy of Adoption Attorneys
Box 33053
Washington, DC 20033-0053
(202) 331-1955

Child Welfare League of America (CWLA)
440 First Street NW Suite 310
Washington, DC 20001-2085
(202) 638-2952
Fax: (202) 638-4004
http://www.cwla.org/
E-mail: webweaver@cwla.org
This is an association of public and private nonprofit agencies that
are involved in child protection, foster care, adoption, family preservation, day care, teen pregnancy prevention, etc. They set standards
of practice, support accreditation of agencies, provide consultation
and training to child welfare professionals, advocate for laws that
benefit children, conduct research, and maintain an extensive library
of professional publications and training materials.

Dave Thomas Foundation for Adoption
(614) 764-3009
http://www.adopt.org/wendy/html

Families Adopting Children Everywhere (FACE)
P. O. Box 28058
Northwood Station
Baltimore, MD 21239
(410) 488-2656
http://longrun.onweb.com/facewelcome.html

This is an education and advocacy group that publishes a bimonthly magazine called *Face Facts,* and provides courses for adoptive families in the Baltimore and Washington, D.C. area (Family Building Through Adoption or FBTA) and an annual conference for families and professionals.

> Families for Russian and Ukrainian Adoption
> P. O. Box 2944
> Merrifield, VA 22116
> (703) 560-6184
> Fax: (301) 474-4516
> http://www.frua.org
> E-mail: FRUAUSA@aol.com

This organization has chapters all over the country and provides information and support to families adopting in Russia or the Ukraine, including an orphanage directory. They have numerous publications and resources lists available and are actively involved in humanitarian aid.

> International Concerns for Children (ICC)
> 911 Cypress Drive
> Boulder, CO 80303
> (303) 494-8333
> http://www.fortnet.org/ICC/

This nonprofit group publishes an annual Report on Intercountry Adoption (with quarterly updates) as well as a photolisting of waiting children around the world. They also provide information about humanitarian aid programs. The Report on Intercountry Adoption contains useful articles as well as information about agencies all over the United States that are working in international adoptions. Counseling services are provided for families seeking to adopt internationally.

Joint Council on International Children's Services (JCICS)
7 Cheverly Circle
Cheverly, MD 20785-3040
(301) 322-1906
http://www.jcics.org

This is a nonprofit membership organization for adoption professionals, advocacy groups, adoptive parent support groups, and others who are involved in international adoption. Members adhere to ethical standards of practice and work together cooperatively to facilitate the adoption of children from other countries. Member agencies are kept informed of new developments in our country or around the world that affect international adoption. Their website is an excellent source of information for agencies or families.

National Adoption Center
1500 Walnut Street, Suite 701
Philadelphia, PA 19102
(215) 735-9988
1-800-TO-ADOPT (862-3678)
http://adopt.org/

This is a nonprofit organization whose mission is to expand adoption opportunities across the United States for special needs children and those from minority cultures. Their publications touch on a variety of topics of interest to all adoptive families. Many of their publications are free. They administer the National Adoption Exchange, a telecommunications network through which waiting children and waiting adoptive families can be matched. They are cosponsors (with Children Awaiting Parents) of Faces of Adoption, an Internet photolisting of children in need of adoption. They have many useful articles and fact sheets available on line through Adoption Quest as well as information about upcoming conferences around the country.

National Adoption Information Clearinghouse (NAIC)
10530 Rosehaven, Suite 400
Fairfax, VA 22030
P. O. Box 1182
Washington, DC 20013-1182
(703) 352-3488
(888) 251-0075
http://www.calib.com/naic
E-mail: naic@calib.com

NAIC is a service of the Children's Bureau, Administration on Children, Youth and Families in the U.S. Department of Health and Human Services. It provides professionals and the general public with information about all aspects of adoption. Most of the publications are free of charge and cover everything from the home study to the specifics of different types of adoption to finalization and life as an adoptive family. NAIC provides literature regarding applicable state and federal laws as well as listings of agencies, attorneys and support groups in each state. Many of their publications are available at the website, or they can be ordered by phone or mail. Information about adoption conferences all over the country is also available through NAIC.

National Council for Adoption (NCFA)
1930 17th Street NW
Washington, DC 20009
(202) 328-1200
http://www.ncfa-usa.org

This is a nonprofit membership organization of adoption agencies which provides a free information packet to anyone interested in adoption. They also publish a number of books and pamphlets, including The Adoption Factbook.

National Council for Single Adoptive Parents
P. O. Box 15084
Chevy Chase, MD 20825
(202) 966-6367
http://www.adopting.org/ncsap.html

This is a nonprofit organization started by adoptive parents in 1973 to provide information, support, and advocacy for single adults seeking to adopt. They publish *The Handbook for Single Adoptive Parents.*

North American Council on Adoptable Children (NACAC)
970 Raymond Avenue, Suite 106
St. Paul, MN 55114-1149
(612) 644-3036
Fax: (612) 644-3036
http://members.aol.com/nacac
E-mail: nacac@aol.com

This is a very large membership organization that provides education and training for adoptive families, professionals, and parent groups, advocacy and research. Their annual conference is held in a different location each year to make it more accessible to families around the country and in Canada. They operate the National Adoption Assistance Training, Resource and Information Network (NAATRIN) through which families and professionals can access information about state and federal laws and policies for adoption subsidies and assistance programs free of charge. They publish a quarterly newsletter, *Adoptalk,* which features articles about legislative issues, adoption, foster care, and much more.

Office of Children's Issues
Bureau of Consular Affairs
U.S. Department of State
Washington, DC 2020-4818
(202) 736-7000
Fax: (202) 647-2835
Autofax: (202) 647-3000
http://travel.state.gov

This is the office which is responsible for issuing visas to children being adopted internationally. They provide written information and telephone assistance with questions related to international adoptions anywhere in the world.

RESOLVE, Inc.
1310 Broadway
Somerville, MA 02144-1731
(617) 623-0744
http://www.resolve.org

This is a support group with chapters in forty-two states. It provides advocacy and education about infertility and adoption to prospective parents.

The Adoption Information Exchange
6619 132nd Avenue NE
Suite 158
Kirkland, WA 98033
http://www.halcyon.com/adoption/exchange.htm
E-mail: dbarnes_ais@halcyon.com

Information on adoption education and resources in the state of Washington.

Single Adoptive Parents for Adoption of Children Everywhere
(SPACE)
6 Sunshine Avenue
Natick, MA 01760
Offers an annual conference for single adoptive parents.

Internet Photolisting Services for Waiting Children:

AASK—Adopt a Special Kid
http://www.aask.org/children.html

The Adoption Exchange
http://www.adoptex.org/

Children Awaiting Parents (publishers of the CAP Book)
700 Exchange Street
Rochester, NY 14608
(716) 232-5110
Fax: (716) 232-22634
http://www.adopt.org/adopt/cap/cap.html
E-mail: cap@eznet.net

Eagle Village Adoption Services (Michigan)
http://www.netonecom.net/~eagle/adopt.html

Faces of Adoption: America's Waiting Children
http://www.nac.adopt.org/adopt

Family and Children Services Opt to Adopt (Mississippi)
http://www.mdhs.state.ms.us/fcs_adopt.html

Florida Child Adoption Program
http://sun6.dms.state.fl.us/cf_web/adopt/photo.html

Hamilton County's (Ohio) Adoptable Children
http://www.hcadopt.org/

Illinois Department of Children and Family Services
http://www.state.il.us/dcfs

Indiana's Adoption Initiative On-Line Registry
http://www.ai.org/fssa/adoption/

Kansas Farmilies for Kids
http://skyways.lib.ks.us/kansan/kfk/index.html

Michigan Adoption Resource Exchange
http://www.mare.org/

Missouri Adoption Photolisting
http://www.state.mo.us/dss/dfs/adopt/plist.htm

New York Adoption Photolisting
http://www.state.ny.us/dss/adopt/adavail.htm#about

Ohio Adoption Photolisting
http://www.state.oh.us/odhs/oapl

Texas Adoption Resource Exchange
http://www.tdprs.state.tx.us/adoption/tare.html

Wednesday's Child (North Carolina)
http://www.wral-tv.com/features/wedchild/

Wisconsin—Special Needs Child of the Month
http://www.dhfs.state.wi.us/dhfs/progserv/html/snchld.html

Photolistings—International Adoptions
Precious in His Sight
http://www.precious.org

Waiting Children of the World
http://rainbowkids.com/waiting/

AdoptionAgencies.Org Photolisting
http://www.adoptionagencies.org/can

These are multiagency listings; many private agencies have their own listings. Check one of the main adoption websites (http://www.adoption.com, http://www.adoption.org, http://www.adopting.com and http://adopting.org) for private agencies with photolistings.

Photolistings for Prospective Adoptive Parents:
Christian Adoption
P. O. Box 720863
Norman, OK 73070
1-800-277-7006
(405) 360-1206
Fax: (405) 360-1942
http://www.christianadoption.com

This is a service that provides an online photolisting of Christian families seeking to adopt.

Adoption Online Connection
8630-M Guilford Road
#211
Columbia, MD 21046
(410) 489-9393
http://www.adoptiononline.com/

Photolistings for adoptive parents are also found at the main adoption websites (http://www.adoption.com, http://www.adoption.org, http://www.adopting.com and http://adopting.org).

Newsletters and Magazines

Adopted Child
P. O. Box 9362
Moscow, ID 83843
(888) 882-1794
Fax: (208) 883-8035
E-mail: lmelina@moscow.com
http://www.raisingadoptedchildren.com

Adoption/Medical News
Adoption Advocates Press
1921 Ohio Street NE
Palm Bay, FL 32907
Dr. Jerri Jenista is the editor

Adoptive Families Magazine
(see Adoptive Families of America in the organizations section)

The Adoption Connections Project
http://www.sover.net/~adopt
E-mail: adopt@sover.net
Support group of women (birth mothers, adoptive mothers, foster mothers, and stepmothers) which has articles and a newsletter.

Children in Common
P. O. Box 9472
Catonsville, MD 21228
(410) 788-6490
Quarterly newsletter for people interested in Eastern European adoption.

Rainbow Kids (online adoption magazine)
http ://www.rainbowkids.com/
Real Moms (online adoption newsletter)
http://www.comunity.com/adoption/realmoms/

Roots & Wings
P. O. Box 577
Hackettstown, NJ 07840
(908) 813-8252
http://www.adopt-usa.com/rootsandwings/

Medical Resources for Families Adopting Internationally:

Dr. Dana Johnson, Director
International Adoption Clinic
The University of Minnesota
Hospital and Clinic
Box 211 *(continued next page)*

(continued from previous page)
420 Delaware Street SE
Minneapolis, MN 55455
(612) 626-2928
1-800-688-5252
http://www.cyfc.umn.edu/Adoptinfo/iac.html
E-mail: jonhs008@maroon.tc.umn.edu

Dr. Laurie C. Miller, Director
The Floating Hospital For Children
New England Medical Center
International Adoption Clinic
Department of Pediatrics
750 Washington Street
Boston, MA 02111
(617) 636-7285
Fax: (617) 636-8388
http://polaris.nemc.org/

Dr. Jerri Jenista
551 Second Street
Ann Arbor, MI 48103
(313) 668-0419
Fax: (313) 668-9492

Dr. Jane Aronson, Director
International Adoption Medical Consultation Services
Winthrop Pediatric Associates
222 Station Plaza North
Suite 611
Mineola, NY 11501 *(continued next page)*

(516) 663-4417 or (516) 663-3727
http://members.aol.com/jaronmink/index.htm/
E-mail: Jaronmink@aol.com

Dr. Andrew Adesman, Director
Schneider's Children's Hospital
Evaluation Center For Adoption
Suite 139
269-01 76th Avenue
New Hyde Park, NY 11040
Telephone: (718) 470-4000
Fax: (718) 343-3578
http://www.adoption.com/adesman

All of these organizations will review medical records and videos for children who are being considered for adoptive placement. Contact them for fees and specific procedures to be followed.

Financial Assistance:

National Adoption Foundation
100 Mill Plain road
Danbury, CT 06811
1-800-448-7061
Provides grants up to $7,500 and low-interest loans through MBNA American Bank up to $25,000.

First Union National Bank of Maryland
502 Hungerford Drive
Rockville, MD 20850
(888) 314-5437

Sources for Books on Adoption Issues:

Celebrate the Child
P.O. Box 13571
Reading, PA 19612-7050
1-800-237-8400 ext. 34
Fax: (504) 328-7050
http://www.celebratechild.com
E-mail: Celbr8chld@aol.com

Perspectives Press: The Infertility and Adoption Publisher
P. O. Box 90318
Indianapolis, IN 46290-0318
(317) 872-3055
http://www.perspectivespress.com
E-mail: ppress@iquest.net

Tapestry Books
P. O. Box 359
Ringoes, NJ -8551-0359
1-800-765-2367
http://www.tapestrybooks.com

USING THE INTERNET FOR ADOPTION RESEARCH OR NETWORKING

The widespread use of computers in homes and businesses around the world has meant that a wealth of information is now available to families who are seeking to adopt or have adopted a child. There has been much debate over the potential harm or benefit of the use of the

Internet by adopting families. In general, the Internet is a tremendous resource. But there are some basic assumptions which must be kept in mind when using the Internet for adoption networking or education.

- *Use the same or higher standards to evaluate information as you would if reading the newspaper.* In order to be an educated consumer, you should still verify facts with several different sources before acting on anything you see. Hopefully, you would do the same thing with brochures or pamphlets you receive in the mail about adoption agencies or other professionals.

- *Consider the source.* Information obtained through any means is only as reliable as the person providing it. The relative anonymity of the Internet makes it possible for some people to distribute false information without consequence. Also, many adoptive families post their personal adoption stories on their websites. These stories are generally a great source of inspiration to others who are considering adoption but you must keep in mind that the opinions and experiences presented may not be representative of other adoption cases.

- *Don't say anything on the Internet that you would not say to someone in person.* If you participate in an electronic mailing list or bulletin board, you will be surprised by the amount of bickering that can go on when certain issues are raised. A topic like working mothers versus stay at home mothers can generate a lot of heated discussion and hurt feelings.

- *Keep in mind that anyone can read what you post on the Internet.* Mailing lists for adoptive families may be monitored from time to time by child welfare officials overseas and others who may be offended by negative comments.

If you are totally new to the Internet, you might want to sign up for an introductory course at your local library or find a friend who can give you some pointers. When you are just getting started, you need to know the basics of how to use search engines, how to bookmark websites that are of interest to you, and how to navigate between websites without losing track of your starting point. It is also helpful to know how to send and receive electronic mail, or E-mail. A little practice and guidance will save you a lot of time and headaches.

One way to get started exploring adoption resources on the Internet is to use a search engine such as Yahoo or AltaVista and enter key words such as "adoption" or "international adoption." The search engine will scan the web for sites that contain those words. This method can be very time-consuming and you can end up with lots of results that are of little interest or use.

Another way is through the general adoption websites. There are several general adoption sites that provide a good starting point for anyone considering adoption. These sites have articles about a wide variety of adoption topics such as open adoption, selecting an agency, international adoption, networking, and much more. They also have links to other sites of interest to adoptive families and birth parents, a forum for posting information about prospective families seeking to adopt a child, search registries, information about adoption organizations, laws in various states, adoption-related books, etc. All of the sites offer information about adoption mailing lists and host chat rooms and bulletin boards where members of the adoption community can communicate with one another. The general adoption sites are:

- Adopt: Assistance, Information and Support—
  http://www.adopting.org

- Adopting.com—http://www.adopting.com
- AdoptioNetwork:—http://www.adoption.org
- Adoption.com—http://www.adoption.com

Another starting point is through a web ring or a series of linked websites. One example is the Adoption Web Ring located at http//www.plumsite.com/adoptionring. When you enter this site, you can choose a list of the ring members and visit only the sites you want, or you can simply click on the next ring button on each site and keep moving through the linked sites until you come back to the beginning. This webring includes personal stories as well as organizations, agencies, and adoption professionals.

Listservs
A listserv is basically a system through which electronic mail or e-mail is distributed to all the members at the same time. In order to join a listserv, you must go to the appropriate website and complete the subscription form or send an e-mail message to a certain address. There are many public listservs available where you simply have to request membership. There are also private lists for which membership is based upon specific criteria such as being a client of a certain adoption agency. Each list is owned or administered by one or more individuals who are responsible for day to day list maintenance. Command messages are generally handled automatically and problems will be directed to the list administrator. When you subscribe to a listserv, you will be given instructions on how to unsubscribe as well as how to change to a digest format, if available. Print out the instructions and keep them in a safe place so you will know how to get off the list if you need to. Due to the fact that your mailbox with your Internet Service

Provider will only hold a certain number of messages, you will want to unsubscribe if you are going out of town and no one else will be checking your e-mail. Some listservs have as many as 1,500 members at any given time and there are hundreds of messages posted each day. If you are subscribing to one of those lists, the digest format, where you receive twenty or thirty messages together rather than hundreds of individual messages can save a lot of time in opening, closing, and deleting messages. You will also receive an explanation of the basic rules of the list and the consequences for violations.

Bulletin Boards

Bulletin boards are forums for posting and reading messages. You can respond to messages, ask new questions, or just browse.

Newsgroups

There are a number of newsgroups which provide lively discussions on adoption issues. Many people find them intimidating since they are largely unmoderated.

Index

Notes